The DNA Code

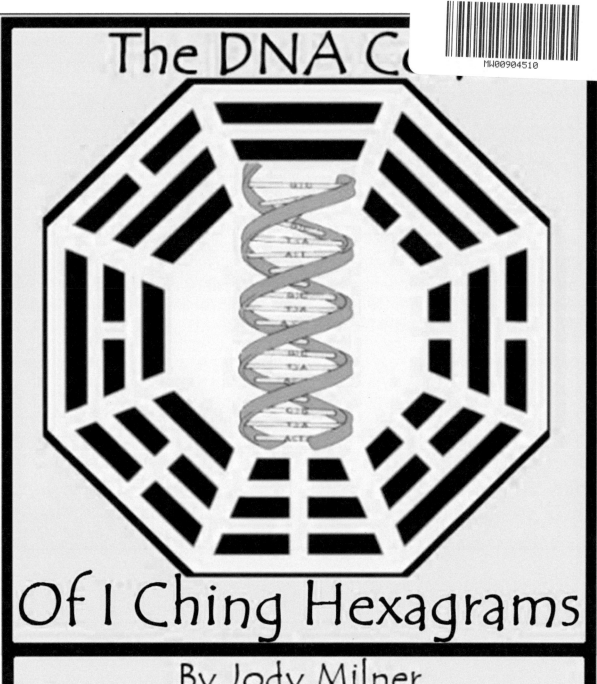

Of I Ching Hexagrams

By Jody Milner

The DNA Code of Earlier Heaven

By Jody Milner

Self-Published by Jody Milner

Jodyelizabeth55@hotmail.com

The DNA Code

Of I Ching Hexagrams

By Jody Milner

Author's Note to the Reader:

My I Ching adventure began in 1989 when an acquaintance handed me a yellow hardback copy of the Wilhelm/Baynes interpretation of the Chinese classic. I had never heard of I Ching and knew very little about Chinese history or philosophy. It was long before the Internet would arrive, so I could not go home and learn about it online. I was pretty much on my own. I left with the book after a brief explanation that it was an ancient Chinese oracle and instruction on how to use the three-penny method when seeking an answer to a question.

I took it home and played around with asking questions of the oracle. The answers it generated were interesting. I read the forward by Carl Jung and found his ideas about the text intriguing. A few days later, I attempted to return it.

"No, no. It's a gift. You keep it," she insisted.

By 2005, I had studied I Ching as an oracle and as Confucian philosophy, but I was not an expert. I had read other Chinese philosophy and history as well and started collecting jade from China via eBay. Then one day, for some unknown reason, I suddenly became obsessed with trying to figure out why and how the hexagrams had been organized in such a way. Much of this effort centered around trigrams. After months of struggle and blocked paths, I finally gave up the quest, but still wholeheartedly believed there was a method behind the organizational madness.

It was not until 2020 that hexagram obsession struck again. One day, out of nowhere, the six points of the Star of David came into my mind. After sketching it, I immediately associated these points with the six lines of the I Ching hexagrams. This time, I began to find success beginning with decoding the eight-house system. This was an important discovery, but also, a difficult place to begin.

Astrologically speaking, having a Venus ruler in Sagittarius coupled with an Aries Mars, I tend toward "enthusiastic optimist in a very big hurry." As I began to decode the secrets locked within the hexagrams, I was often overwhelmed with excitement and thankfulness over my discoveries. I quickly taught myself how to use Amazon KDP and self-published versions of my work.

I now realize that my first publication attempt, *Code of the Dragon King*, was highly unreadable. Although it contained some ground-breaking information, I apologize to those few kind souls who bought it for its poor organization. My second attempt, *Secrets of I Ching Revealed*, was an improvement, and many thanks to those who bought or read it. Still, when I settled down, I could see it required work.

My third book was far more concise and readable. Also, I kept discovering new information and wanted to share it with anyone who might be interested. Book three added information about the genetic code and how it links up with the sixty-four-hexagram system. It still was not complete and another premature release.

In my latest endeavor, I show the reader, step-by-step, the method which decodes the Earlier Heaven trigram wheel into an eight-house system and ultimately, into a genetic codon map. How this amazing artifact found its way into the heart and soul of Chinese culture before 2000 BC, remains a historical mystery.

What I have discovered, however, after unlocking the Earlier Heaven hidden code, assures me it is the key to our own genetic DNA patterns.

My present book begins with the step-by-step decoding process which unlocks the mathematics of the genetic code. It includes all my recent unpublished work, explanations, and the resulting charts. The second part of this book is made up of relevant chapters from my third book so that those who did not read it will have access to all information I have yet uncovered. This information includes King Wen's method of organizing the hexagrams into their present order, the house systems, geometry, and the pyramid connection.

Thanks for your interest in my work.

Jody Milner

Table of Contents

1: Origins of the Oracle

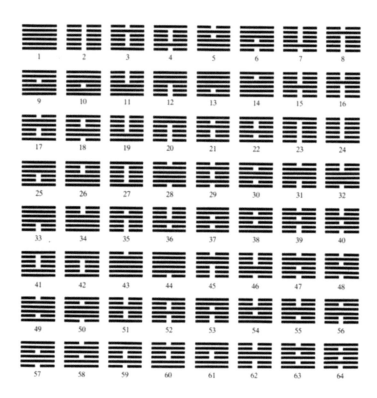

I Ching, or *Book of Changes*, is considered the first of the Chinese classics. It is an ancient oracle built on a sixty-four-hexagram system. Each hexagram has an associated chapter which includes its numerical position, the title of the hexagram, a judgment, a metaphorical image, and an additional commentary for each of the six stacked lines. The inquirer typically writes down a question, then uses one of several methods to obtain a six-line stack of broken and/or solid lines. For example, hexagram 2 has the title K'un, or The Receptive. All six of its lines are broken, or yin lines. In this hexagram the judgment metaphorically relates the behavior of a mare to the behavior of a human, pointing out favorable and unfavorable choices a person might make. The image discusses the receptive condition of earth and how receptivity can be beneficial. The commentary on each line might point to a positive, neutral, or negative outcome.

The foundational principle of *I Ching* is yin and yang, or duality. In fact, the entire trigram-hexagram system is built on the basic idea of these opposing or complimentary forces. Trigrams and hexagrams are composed of two types of lines. These are broken yin lines and solid yang lines. There are many characteristics which, through at least three millennia, have come to be associated with yin and yang. Some of the most common are earth/heaven, dark/light, empty/full, cold/hot, and female/male. It is amazing how these two line-types have acquired so much information.

The story of *I Ching* begins with the Earlier Heaven trigram wheel as pictured above. Because this pictographic artifact dates back into prehistory, its origins are shrouded in mystery, myth, and folklore. I have read it dates as far back as 3000 BC, but its most accepted beginning point is about 2600 BC. Around this time, a king named Fu Xi, along with his sister Nuwa, helped the Chinese people establish a patriarchal society by creating the institution of marriage. From that point forward, the family unit would be the primary social entity in China. Fu Xi is also credited with establishing agriculture, improvement of fishing and hunting methods, and assisting with flood control.

Especially important, it is believed Fu Xi introduced the Earlier Heaven wheel of eight trigrams that would eventually become the famed Chinese classic, *Book of Changes*, or *I Ching* as it is known in the western world.

Nuwa and Fuxi depicted on Chinese murals of the Wu Liang shrines, Han dynasty (206 BC – 220 AD). (Miuki / Public Domain)

The following words honoring him are carved onto one of the columns at the Fuxi Temple in Gansu Province "...Then came Fu Xi and looked upward and contemplated the images in the heavens and looked downward and contemplated the occurrences on earth. He united man and wife, regulated the five stages of change, and laid down the laws of humanity. He devised the eight trigrams in order to gain mastery over the world."

Some writings depict Fu Xi as a dragon king responsible for creating the trigrams. Other writing credits Fu Xi with having received the trigrams from a dragon river-god. The trigrams were either delivered on the shell of a river tortoise or conceived of while viewing a river tortoises shell.

Looking at the octagonal wheel, it is highly reminiscent of a tortoise shell. Taken together, the above clues lead me to believe Fu Xi found an ancient artifact depicting the trigram wheel which had been washed up by a flood.

2: Decoding Earlier Heaven Trigram Wheel

The following paragraphs explain my present working hypothesis concerning the origin and evolution of the I Ching hexagrams and oracle.

A combination of Chinese history and mythology points to the "Earlier Heaven" trigram wheel as the progenitor from which everything "I Ching" later evolved. Fu Xi, a ruler predating 2000 BC, is the first person associated with this ancient artifact. It seems that during his heroic work at flood control on the Yellow River, the river dragon sent him a tortoise with the image of the eight trigrams. My interpretation of this myth is that during a cleanup after a great flood, an (already ancient) artifact of the trigram wheel was unearthed. Because the artifact had been churned up, or pushed downstream, by the flood, it was considered a gift of the river dragon. Additionally, because the octagonal shape of the trigram wheel is reminiscent of a tortoise shell, and because the line markings resemble those seen on tortoise shells, the unearthed artifact became forever identified as having arrived on the back of a river tortoise.

What significance or hidden mystery did the artifact hold? How did the early discoverers of the trigram wheel answer these questions before incorporating the trigrams into their traditional culture and rituals? There is one clue which comes in the way of animal bones and tortoise shells. Many of these had been purposely burned in fires until surface cracks formed. Pits containing the relics have been unearthed during modern times. On many of the bones and shells, there is an early form of script. The script is assumed to be written questions, and the fire-caused cracks are assumed to be the responses to the queries.

The burned and cracked bones and shells have been linked to the trigrams. The idea is that this early culture had assigned meaning to the trigrams and then used the cracking of bones and shells as an oracle for seeking future outcomes and answers to problems. This idea makes perfect sense, as even today people tend to bestow mythological, ritual, or magical properties to ancient information they cannot completely understand.

Once discovered, the question is why and how were the trigrams assembled into hexagrams? My personal experience with the Earlier Heaven trigram wheel and its resulting hexagrams has shown me they are an intuitive/instructional knowledge system.

Theoretically a contemplative individual could assemble the "Earlier Heaven" trigram wheel by logically considering the two types of lines, broken and solid, of which it is composed. Simply beginning with the possibilities inherent in a broken and a solid line, the four emblems, or couplets, can be formed. They are the only four possibilities and look like this.

Lines and Emblems

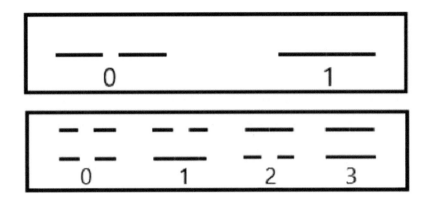

Next, one could decide to increase the stacked lines to sets of three. Again, I am not sure why such a grouping of triple lines would be created, unless one were assembling a counting method. In this case, a set of three-line stacks consisting only of broken and solid lines could result in a binary numeral set using 0's and 1's. Looking at the above emblems from left to right, we see 0, 1, 2, and 3. Pictures of 0 to 3 would not be a very satisfactory result if that is as far as one could go. Adding a third line to the stack gives a total of 8 numerals, from 0 through 7. Because it is a closed set, it is still not a very satisfactory result if considering trigrams as numerals and only slightly superior to tally marks.

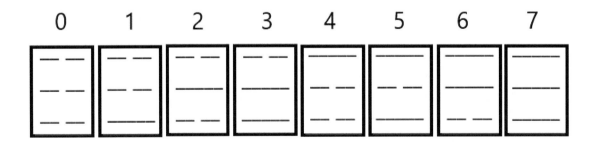

Reasons for their creation aside, at this point an interesting feature of the trigrams emerges. The eight possible trigrams can be paired up as four binary, or line-to-line opposite pairs. Using the counting system above, these opposites always add up to seven when considered as numbers. When the trigrams are numerically assembled into an octagonal pattern of line-to-line opposites, the results must be a split numeric system. This pattern is also how the Earlier Heaven, or original, trigram wheel embedded into the culture of Fu Xi.

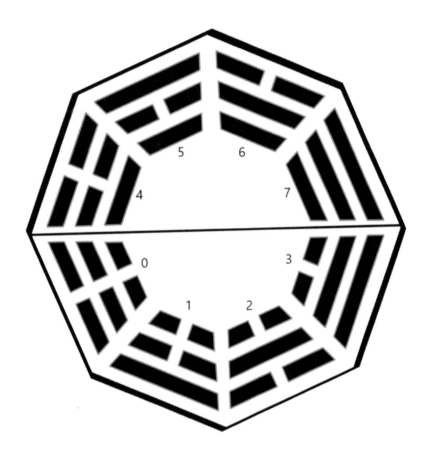

Although just how the Earlier Heaven trigram wheel came to be created remains a mystery, this intuitive and instructional wheel points directly to the idea of pairing the eight trigrams to form hexagrams. It does not ask for three or more trigrams to be stacked together. It directly points to the method of pulling pairs of trigrams to center to merge them into sets of six lines. Because it is a highly organized system of patterns, I looked for any obvious technical clues when pairing the trigrams at center. The following wheels show the intuitive method I discovered. Using this precise method of pairing trigrams into hexagrams resulted in the eight houses I had already found using another, far more complicated method. After discovering the eight-house system, I realized if the trigram wheel, as found in its earliest form, is a legitimate key which unlocks a binary code, the wheel alone must contain all relevant information.

Other than the first house set, which are primary because they pair at center with themselves and are the same from top-to-bottom or bottom-to-top, all other pairs flip to form an alternate hexagram. This necessitates eight sets of eight hexagrams. In the I Ching text, King Wen arranged the hexagrams into these flipped pairs. For the eight primary hexagrams which have no flipped pair, he paired them as line-to-line opposite pairs.

The resulting house sets look like the following. There is an organized pattern of flipped pairs and line-to-line opposite pairs within each group, but they are somewhat difficult to perceive in this format.

The hexagrams needed to be assigned logical designations or labels so they could be more easily be compared and discussed, each as an independent pattern. But how? This brings back the idea of the four emblems, or couplets, as show earlier. When I added the numeric lables of 0, 1, 2, or 3 to the the three emblems which compose each hexagram, obvious patterns of relationships within and between the hexagrams and houses emerged.

0,0,0	2,0,1	1,0,2	3,0,3	0,3,0	2,3,1	1,3,2	3,3,3
2,0,0	0,0,1	3,0,2	1,0,3	2,3,0	0,3,1	3,3,2	1,3,3
1,0,0	3,0,1	0,0,2	2,0,3	1,3,0	3,3,1	0,3,2	2,3,3
3,0,0	1,0,1	2,0,2	0,0,3	3,3,0	1,3,1	2,3,2	0,3,3
0,2,0	2,2,1	1,2,2	3,2,3	0,1,0	2,1,1	1,1,2	3,1,3
2,2,0	0,2,1	3,2,2	1,2,3	2,1,0	0,1,1	3,1,2	1,1,3
1,2,0	3,2,1	0,2,2	2,2,3	1,1,0	3,1,1	0,1,2	2,1,3
3,2,0	1,2,1	2,2,2	0,2,3	3,1,0	1,1,1	2,1,2	0,1,3

For example, four of the house sets have 0 and 3 as their center emblem and the other four have 1 and 2 as their center. Emblem pairs of line-to-line opposite hexagrams always add up to 3, 3, 3. Lower and upper emblems within a house set are always two sets of 0, 1, 2, 3. Within a house, upper, middle, and lower emblems always total 12.

The next logical step was to sequence the hexagrams according to their emblems, which is shown in the next chart. This was accomplished by beginning the counting with the bottom couplet sequence of 000, 001, 002, 003, then moving to 1 in the central couplet and again sequencing the bottom set, 010, 011, 012, 013. Once placed into sequential order according to emblems, they were given a numeric lable. As it logically turned out, when beginning with zero and proceeding through sixty-three, these lables correlate to each hexagram's binary numeric value when adding from the bottom up. I kept the color coding as house identifiers.

Organizing by Emblems

000	001	002	003	010	011	012	013
0	1	2	3	4	5	6	7
020	021	022	023	030	031	032	033
8	9	10	11	12	13	14	15
100	101	102	103	110	111	112	113
16	17	18	19	20	21	22	23
120	121	122	123	130	131	132	133
24	25	26	27	28	29	30	31
200	201	202	203	210	211	212	213
32	33	34	35	36	37	38	39
220	221	222	223	230	231	232	233
40	41	42	43	44	45	46	47
300	301	302	303	310	311	312	313
48	49	50	51	52	53	54	55
320	321	322	323	330	331	332	333
56	57	58	59	60	61	62	63

The binary values are counted as shown in the tables below. Solid lines begin with a value of one on the first line and double in value moving up the ladder. One can add up the individual line values of a hexagram or memorize the values of the upper and lower trigrams and add up the trigram pair. In the trigram value chart, top values are for the upper trigrams and the bottom values are for the lower trigrams.

Hexagram Line Values		
— —	0	——— 32
— —	0	——— 16
— —	0	——— 8
— —	0	——— 4
— —	0	——— 2
— —	0	——— 1

Trigram Value Chart

0+0+0=0	8+0+0=8	0+16+0=16	8+16+0=24
0+0+0=0	1+0+0=1	0+2+0=2	1+2+0=3
0+0+32=32	8+0+32=40	0+16+32=48	8+16+32=56
0+0+4+4	1+0+4=5	0+2+4=6	1+2+4=7

Looking at the sequenced eight by eight grid above, I soon noticed the distinct color pattern of the primary and complimentary houses. When I removed everything other than the yellow and green house groups, I was left with the following pattern. These are the houses that start with binary values of 0 and 7.

000 (0)							013 (7)
			023 (11)	030 (12)			
		102 (18)			111 (21)		
	121 (25)					132 (30)	
	201 (33)					212 (38)	
		222 (42)			231 (45)		
			303 (51)	310 (52)			
320 (56)							333 (63)

I then looked for other color-coded patterns. It turned out that the houses beginning with 1 and 6 patterned together, as well as 2 with 5 and 3 with 4 as shown below.

001 1 — 012 6
022 10 — 031 13
103 19 — 110 20
120 24 — 133 31
200 32 — 213 39
223 43 — 230 44
302 50 — 311 53
321 57 — 332 62

002 2 — 011 5
021 9 — 032 14
100 16 — 113 23
123 27 — 130 28
203 35 — 210 36
220 40 — 233 47
301 49 — 312 54
322 58 — 331 61

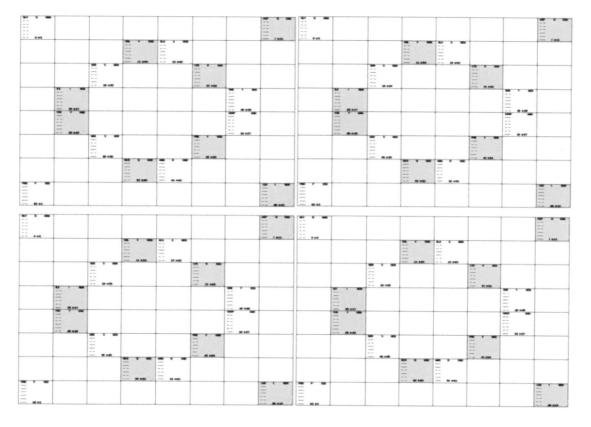

Eventually, I realized the four grids were all making the same pattern. I tiled each grid into groups of four to reveal that each of the house pairs created an identical pattern to the yellow and green pair. The sets of four are shown below.

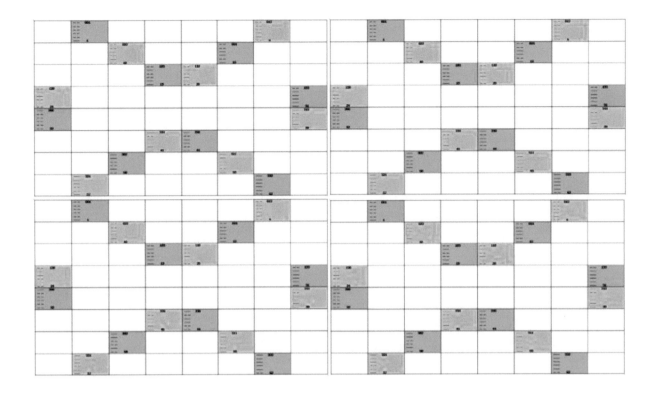
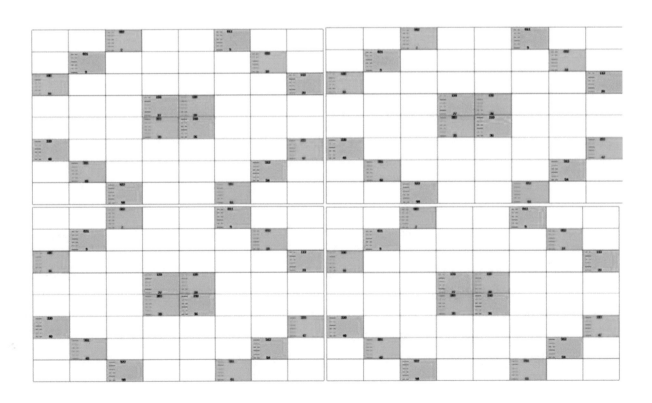

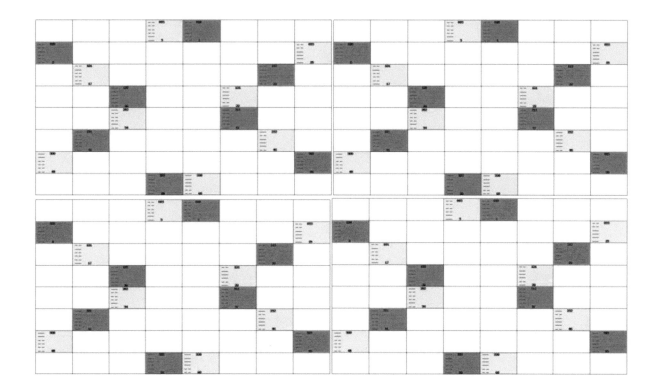

Next, I picked up and moved each sixteen-hexagram pattern into its own eight-by-eight grid. Because the yellow primary and green complimentary houses were already centered in their correct positions, I only needed to move the other three sets. This resulted in what I called the position charts. Each hexagram has its own position. This results in each of the sixteen positions having four hexagrams which can occupy it.

000 — 0						013 — 7
		023 — 11	030 — 12			
	102 — 18			111 — 21		
	121 — 25				132 — 30	
	201 — 33				212 — 38	
	222 — 42			231 — 45		
		303 — 51	310 — 52			
320 — 56						333 — 63

213 — 39						200 — 32
		230 — 44	223 — 43			
		311 — 53		302 — 50		
	332 — 62				321 — 57	
	012 — 6				001 — 1	
	031 — 13		022 — 10			
		110 — 20	103 — 19			
133 — 31						120 — 24

Top grid

205 / 35							210 / 36
			220 / 40	233 / 47			
		301 / 49			312 / 54		
	322 / 58					331 / 61	
	002 / 2					011 / 5	
		021 / 9			032 / 14		
			100 / 16	113 / 23			
123 / 27							130 / 28

Bottom grid

010 / 4							002 / 3
			022 / 15	020 / 8			
		112 / 22			101 / 17		
	131 / 29					122 / 26	
	211 / 37					202 / 34	
		232 / 46			221 / 41		
			313 / 55	300 / 48			
330 / 60							323 / 59

Next, I arranged these four into a series as shown below. This pattern is highly reminiscent of the double-helix of the DNA code upon which all earthly life is built.

0							7	39						32	35					40	47				4				15	8		3
		11	12						44	43									40	47								15	8			
	18			21				53			50					49			54					22			17					
25					30		62				57		58				61				29				26							
33					38		6				1		2			5					37				34							
	42			45				13			10			9			14					46		41								
		51	52						20	19						16	23							55	48							
56							63	31						24	27						28	60					59					

After having earlier discovered the eight houses, geometry, magic squares, and pyramid blueprints as coded within the hexagrams of *I Ching*, I believed I had completed my work. I had documented these findings in my previous books. Then one day, while continuing to investigate *I Ching* on the internet, I stumbled across an image connecting hexagrams to our genetic code. It was included as additional material in a PDF of "James Legge, translation, Sacred Books of the East, vol. 16 [1899]" https://ornasonova.com/I-Ching.pdf.

I was immediately intrigued by the image. A part of that image is included below. The hexagrams were arranged into a binary sequenced split-system, just as I had arranged them on my own.

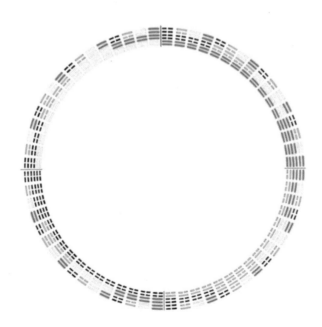

I was especially interested in the dissection of hexagrams into three, color-coded, two-line emblems. I had previously explored parts of the 1973 book, *The I Ching & The Genetic Code* by Dr. Martin Schonberger, specifically about hexagrams being considered in relationship to genetics. However, not being a geneticist, I didn't make much sense of it at the time. Also, like everything else about *I Ching*, authors want to connect the mathematical patterns and science to the mysticism of the meanings assigned to the sixty-four hexagrams. This quickly muddies the water, in my opinion. The symbolic meanings for the hexagrams were most likely written or compiled by King Wen around 1000 BC, more than one thousand years after the discovery of Earlier Heaven trigram wheel.

Soon after finding the image highlighting the emblem triplets, I began a limited study of codon charts, DNA and RNA coding, proteins, amino acids, and their alignments. As I am not an expert in genetics, I am not going to attempt to instruct the reader in DNA science. I am here to point out the similarity between the patterns inherent in both the sixty-four hexagrams and the sixty-four possible codon groupings. The following is a circular codon chart as found in many forms, both round and square, on the internet. I like this one because it includes the amino acid abbreviations.

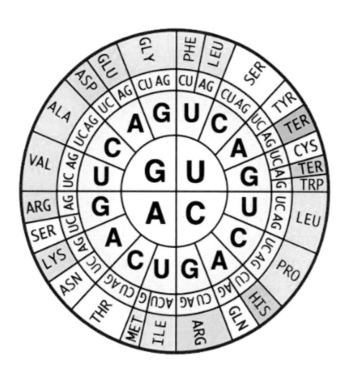

Using the four-color scheme for emblems, as cited above, I rotated the circle to represent the lower and upper hemispheres of a binary split-system as in my previous Earlier Heaven maps. Gradually, I arrived at the following chart. It is organized by the same emblem code sequence which is also the binary numeric sequence.

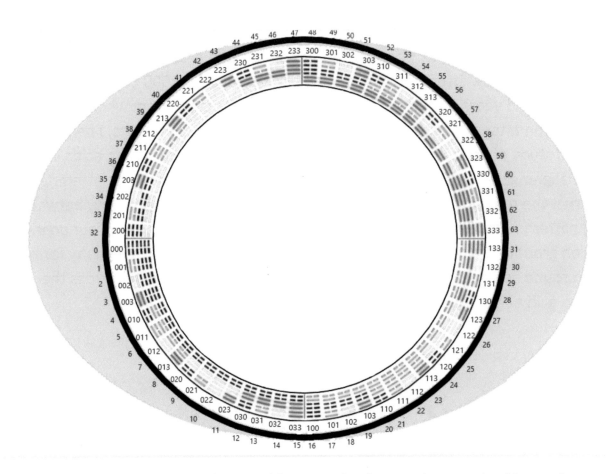

Next, I connected the four emblems to the four codons, as had been done on the internet site provided above. In the following chart, I added the codon letter abbreviations and the amino acids alongside the corresponding hexagrams. The color-coded emblems help with ease of reading. Black represents two broken lines, or 0. Blue represents a solid line under a broken line, or 1. Yellow represents a broken line under a solid line, or 2. Pink represents two solid lines, or 3. Black 0 pairs with pink 3, and blue 1 pairs with yellow 2. Emblem pairs always total 3.

On the hexagram wheel, each hexagram's binary value is directly across from its binary partner. The wheel is split and moving in opposite directions numerically from 0 and from 32, and opposing hexagram always add up to 63.

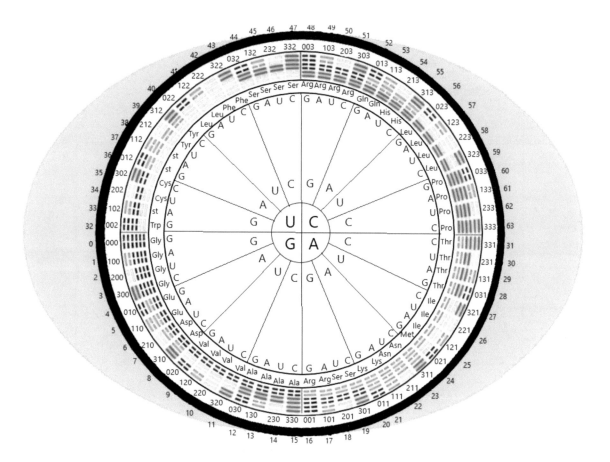

Now that the element of genetic coding has been added, we will return to the position charts. Of course, there is no definitive way to decern codons and amino acids from Earlier Heaven trigram wheel. It is simply the mathematics of the DNA code.

After decoding the sixteen pattern-positions of the sixty-four hexagrams, as previously shown in the pattern charts, I assembled them into one pattern chart for clarity.

0 = 000 GLY 39 = 213 TYR 35 = 203 CYS 4 = 010 GLU 78 total							7 = 013 ASP 32 = 200 TRP 36 = 210 stop 3 = 003 GLY 78 total
			11 = 023 VAL 44 = 230 SER 40 = 220 LEU 15 = 033 ALA 110 total	12 = 030 ALA 43 = 223 PHE 47 = 233 SER 8 = 020 VAL 110 total			
		18 = 102 SER 53 = 311 GLN 49 = 301 ARG 22 = 112 ASN 142 total			21 = 111 LYS 50 = 302 ARG 54 = 312 HIS 17 = 101 ARG 142 total		
	25 = 121 ILE 62 = 332 PRO 58 = 322 LEU 29 = 131 THR 174 total					30 = 132 THR 57 = 321 LEU 61 = 331 PRO 26 = 122 ILE 174 total	
	33 = 201 stop 6 = 012 ASP 2 = 002 GLY 37 = 211 stop 78 total					38 = 212 TYR 1 = 001 GLY 5 = 011 GLU 34 = 202 CSY 78 total	
		42 = 222 PHE 13 = 031 ALA 9 = 021 VAL 46 = 232 SER 110 total			45 = 231 SER 10 = 022 VAL 14 = 032 ALA 41 = 221 LEU 110 total		
			51 = 303 ARG 20 = 110 LYS 16 = 100 ARG 55 = 313 HIS 142 total	52 = 310 GLN 19 = 103 SER 23 = 113 ASN 48 = 300 ARG 142 total			
56 = 320 LEU 31 = 133 THR 27 = 123 ILE 60 = 330 PRO 174 total							63 = 333 PRO 24 = 120 MET 28 = 130 THR 59 = 323 LEU 174 total

Next, I closely examined the binary grid for any new clues as to how to proceed with utilizing the patterns. I created the following grid with added positions to further orient my perspective.

ROW #	COLUMN 0	COLUMN 1	COLUMN 2	COLUMN 3	COLUMN 4	COLUMN 5	COLUMN 6	COLUMN 7
1	000 P-0 — 0 GLY	001 P-58 — 1 GLY	002 P-35 — 2 GLY	003 P-7 — 3 GLY	010 P-0 — 4 GLU	011 P-58 — 5 GLU	012 P-35 — 6 ASP	013 P-7 — 7 ASP
2	020 P-12 — 8 VAL	021 P-42 — 9 VAL	022 P-45 — 10 VAL	023 P-11 — 11 VAL	030 P-12 — 12 ALA	031 P-42 — 13 ALA	032 P-45 — 14 ALA	033 P-11 — 15 ALA
3	100 P-51 — 16 ARG	101 P-21 — 17 ARG	102 P-18 — 18 SER	103 P-52 — 19 SER	110 P-51 — 20 LYS	111 P-21 — 21 LYS	112 P-18 — 22 ASN	113 P-52 — 23 ASN
4	120 P-63 — 24 MET	121 P-25 — 25 ILE	122 P-30 — 26 ILE	123 P-56 — 27 ILE	130 P-63 — 28 THR	131 P-25 — 29 THR	132 P-30 — 30 THR	133 P-56 — 31 THR
5	200 P-7 — 32 TRP	201 P-33 — 33 STOP	202 P-58 — 34 CYS	203 P-0 — 35 CYS	210 P-7 — 36 STOP	33 — 211 P- — 37 STOP	212 P-58 — 38 TYR	213 P-0 — 39 TYR
6	220 P-11 — 40 LEU	221 P-45 — 41 LEU	222 P-42 — 42 PHE	223 P-12 — 43 PHE	230 P-11 — 44 SER	231 P-45 — 45 SER	232 P-42 — 46 SER	233 P-12 — 47 SER
7	300 P-52 — 48 ARG	301 P-18 — 49 ARG	302 P-21 — 50 ARG	303 P-51 — 51 ARG	310 P-52 — 52 GLN	311 P-18 — 53 GLN	312 P-21 — 54 HIS	313 P-51 — 55 HIS
8	320 P-56 — 56 LEU	321 P-30 — 57 LEU	322 P-25 — 58 LEU	323 P-63 — 59 LEU	330 P-56 — 60 PRO	331 P-30 — 61 PRO	332 P-25 — 62 PRO	333 P-63 — 63 PRO

I found that every four-by-four hexagram group contained one of each of the sixteen positions. Although it was a tedious process, I documented each sixteen-hexagram set. There are sixty-four unique sets. Then I began assembling the sets into individual position charts. I soon realized that each set has its own binary-compliment set. I assembled these into paired sets, flipping and mirroring images of the second set so that all binary opposites align. I will include all sets and paired sets in the next chapters but will first show explanatory examples.

Column 0, 1st Row

000 P-0	001 P-68	002 P-69	003 P-7
0 GLY	1 GLY	2 GLY	3 GLY
020 P-12	021 P-42	022 P-45	023 P-11
8 VAL	9 VAL	10 VAL	11 VAL
100 P-61	101 P-21	102 P-18	103 P-52
16 ARG	17 ARG	18 SER	19 SER
120 P-63	121 P-25	122 P-30	123 P-56
24 MET	25 ILE	26 ILE	27 ILE

Column 4, 5th Row

210 P-7	211 P-69	212 P-68	213 P-0
36 STOP	37 STOP	38 TYR	39 TYR
230 P-11	231 P-45	232 P-42	233 P-12
44 SER	45 SER	46 SER	47 SER
310 P-52	311 P-18	312 P-21	313 P-61
52 GLN	53 GLN	54 HIS	55 HIS
330 P-56	331 P-30	332 P-25	333 P-63
60 PRO	61 PRO	62 PRO	63 PRO

When comparing the two four-by-four sets it can be observed that column 0, 1st row is a flipped mirror matchup of column 4, 5th row. They are composed of binary opposites. Binary opposite pairs add up to 63. In fact, there is only one set 4 x 4 set which matches up with another. This means that there is correct binary codon alignment for all 16 positions. All A's aligns with T/U's, and G's align with C's. The following is the paired position charts of the above paired groups.

Column 0, 1st Row

000 P-0 / 0 GLY							003 P-7 / 3 GLY
			023 P-11 / 11 VAL	020 P-12 / 8 VAL			
		102 P-18 / 18 SER			101 P-21 / 17 ARG		
	121 P-25 / 25 ILE					122 P-30 / 26 ILE	
	002 P-33 / 2 GLY					001 P-38 / 1 GLY	
		021 P-42 / 9 VAL			022 P-45 / 10 VAL		
			100 P-51 / 16 ARG	103 P-52 / 19 SER			
123 P-56 / 27 ILE							120 P-63 / 24 MET

Column 4, 5th Row

333 P-63 / 63 PRO							330 P-56 / 60 PRO
			310 P-52 / 52 GLN	313 P-51 / 55 HIS			
		231 P-45 / 45 SER			232 P-42 / 46 SER		
	212 P-38 / 38 TYR					211 P-33 / 37 STOP	
	331 P-30 / 61 PRO					332 P-25 / 62 PRO	
		312 P-21 / 54 HIS			311 P-18 / 53 GLN		
			233 P-12 / 47 SER	230 P-11 / 44 SER			
210 P-7 / 36 STOP							213 P-0 / 39 TYR

Now imagine this pair as three-dimensionally side-by-side rather than stacked on a flat surface. The double helix, as coded in the Earlier Heaven trigram wheel becomes clear.

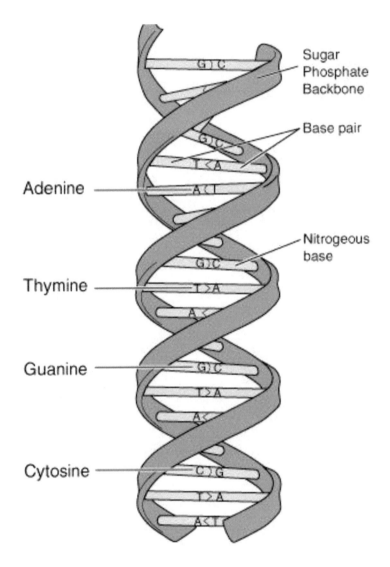

Public Domain Image

Once the code of Earlier Heaven trigram wheel has been fully unlocked, it can be put away and replaced with the eight-by-eight grid and the split-system hexagram wheel it revealed. Everything presented here, other than the names of codons and amino acids, can be directly decoded from this ancient artifact.

The entire decoding process, as presented, can be accomplished directly from studying the Earlier Heaven trigram wheel. The resulting patterns are fascinating, but the central question remains. Why was the octagonal trigram wheel created? What is the original purpose of the hexagram language it encodes?

I wanted to take the reader on a step-by-step journey through the decoding of the Earlier Heaven trigram wheel which took years of time, determination, and patience to fully grasp. However, on its own it contains all the mathematical information I have described.

3: Solving King Wen's Puzzle

Reign: 1100 – 1050 BC

  My inquiry into hexagrams began as a curiosity centered on King Wen's long-standing organization of the hexagrams. Intuitively, I knew there had to be a method behind the seeming madness of the book order. The first important clue came from delving deeply into the three natural pair-type displayed by hexagrams. The final clue, which opened the door to the mystery came when I arranged the hexagrams into a numeric binary chart. I do not believe King Wen perceived the hexagrams as numeric, but he did use their binary-pairing feature extensively in his writing.

  There is no definitive knowledge concerning what the trigrams had come to mean during the 1500 plus years before he wrote the first Chinese classic. Nor do we know if the trigrams had been combined into hexagrams. It is possible that King Wen's genius was in stacking the trigrams into the sixty-four possible forms and assigning them meanings.

  What I discovered is that King Wen first organized the hexagrams into the natural thirty-two binary, or line-to-line, opposites. Looking at these complimentary pairs, he then assigned them titles and images. Next, he reorganized them into flip-pairs. Finally, he ordered the new pairs into the "received" book sequence. Additionally, he further obscured the process by switching two of the pairs with one another. The following images will clarify his method.

First, we will look at the three types of pairs inherent in the hexagrams. There are four primary pairs totaling eight hexagrams, four complimentary pairs also totaling eight hexagrams, and twenty-four flip pairs totaling the remaining 48 hexagrams. These are the pairs used in the book layout. Every hexagram has a binary, or line-to-line, pairing, but Wen only used them in the book sequence when there was no other option.

The primary pairs are easy to spot. They are line-to-line opposites. There is another, less obvious characteristic of primary pairs. They are palindromes. In other words, they are in the same order from top to bottom or bottom to top. All four of the primary pairs are palindromes and therefore, cannot form flip pairs. This is an important clue to the King Wen book order because he had to keep the primary pairs together.

The four complimentary pairs are also line-to-line opposites and were kept together in the book; however, they are not palindromes. Instead, each can be flipped upside down to form the pair partner. There are no other possible partners for either primary or complimentary pairs.

The largest group of pairs in the book order are top to bottom flips of partners. There are 4 Primary pairs totaling 8 hexagrams, 4 Complimentary pairs also totaling 8 hexagrams, and 24 flip pairs totaling the remaining 48 hexagrams.

4 Primary Pairs Or 8 Hexagrams	——— Ken 27 — — — — — — — — ——— Chen	— — Tui 28 ——— ——— ——— Sun ——— — —
4 Complimentary Pairs Or 8 Hexagrams	— — K'un 11 ——— — — ——— Ch'ien ——— ———	——— Ch'ien 12 ——— ——— — — K'un — — — —
24 Flip Pairs Or 48 Hexagrams	— — Tui 31 ——— ——— ——— Ken — — — —	— — Chen 32 — — — — ——— Sun ——— — —

Even before I embraced the hexagrams as binary numerals, I discovered the key which unlocks the eight houses. By studying the pair-types highlighted in the book order, I had already assembled the eight Primary hexagrams and the eight

Complimentary hexagrams into their two respective houses. Next, I combined the 24 flip pairs into 12 groups by partnering them with their line-to-line opposites. Hexagrams 3 and 4 are flips, as are 50 and 49. Hexagrams 3 and 50 are line-to-line opposites as are 4 and 49. In this way, they form natural sets of four. The lower set of four hexagrams behave in precisely the same way. Later in the book I will further explain the method for pairing up the twelve sets of four hexagrams into the six flip pair houses.

3	4	50	49
9	10	16	15

It wasn't until I embraced the hexagrams as binary that I managed to decipher the organization of Wen's ancient puzzle. While studying the hexagrams in a binary numeric grid, it became clear that the smallest numbers and their binary opposites composed the outer ring.

In this eight-by-eight grid, hexagrams are sequenced by their binary value. Book order numbers are on top, binary values are on bottom. Using a color-coding method, I recognized that all hexagrams, aside from 3 and 4, having the lowest book order numbers of 1 through 16 were situated around the outer edge of the grid. Additionally, their line-to-line opposite pairs are also in the outer ring. It turns out that the outer edge of the grid contains all possible hexagrams with at least one fully yin or one fully yang trigram. It then became obvious that King Wen had switched hexagram pair 3 and 4 with pair 19 and 20 to further cover up his organizational method.

2 / 8	24 / 1	7 / 2	19 / 3	15 / 4	36 / 5	46 / 6	11 / 7
16 / 8	51 / 9	40 / 10	54 / 11	62 / 12	55 / 13	32 / 14	34 / 15
8 / 16	3 / 17	29 / 18	60 / 19	39 / 20	63 / 21	48 / 22	5 / 23
45 / 24	17 / 25	47 / 26	58 / 27	31 / 28	49 / 29	28 / 30	43 / 31
23 / 32	27 / 33	4 / 34	41 / 35	52 / 36	22 / 37	18 / 38	26 / 39
35 / 40	21 / 41	64 / 42	38 / 43	56 / 44	30 / 45	50 / 46	14 / 47
20 / 48	42 / 49	59 / 50	61 / 51	53 / 52	37 / 53	57 / 54	9 / 55
12 / 56	25 / 57	6 / 58	10 / 59	33 / 60	13 / 61	44 / 62	1 / 63

The image below shows the hexagram titles, as interpreted by Wilhelm/Baynes. The upper section contains the all-yin/all-yang trigram group of twenty-eight hexagrams. Each hexagram is beside its line-to-line opposite which is also part of the all-yin/all-yang trigram group. King Wen's sequencing pattern becomes clear when looking at the hexagrams from this viewpoint.

He organized all the flip hexagrams into their natural pair groups of four. He then paired each set of 4 with another set of four, creating six sets of eight. I think of these groups as the King Wen houses. Because the Primary and Complimentary hexagrams only come in sets of two, they form their own two houses with eight hexagrams in each. King Wen, therefore, ended up with eight houses with each containing eight hexagrams. Once he completed the pattern, he began the numbering process with the only all Yin/Yang Primary pair as hexagrams 1 and 2. He obviously considered these pure forms as especially important. He numbers the Complimentary all Yin/Yang pair as 11 and 12 to mimic the 1 and 2.

Line Opposite Pairs With K'un, Ch'ien		Titles of Wilhelm/Baynes Title Interpretations of *I Ching*	
1	2	1. Ch'ien / The Creative	2. K'un / The Receptive
19 (3)	33	19. (3) Approach	33. Retreat
20 (4)	34	20. (4) Contemplation (View)	34. The Power of the Great
5	35	5. Waiting (Nourishment)	35. Progress
6	36	6. Conflict	36. Darkening of the Light
7	13	7. The Army	13. Fellowship with Men
8	14	8. Holding Together [Union]	14. Possession in Great Measure
9	16	9. The Taming Power of the Small	16. Enthusiasm
10	15	10. Treading [Conduct]	15. Modesty
11	12	11. Peace	12. Standstill [Stagnation]
23	43	23. Splitting Apart	43. Break-through (Resoluteness)
24	44	24. Return (The Turning Point)	44. Coming to Meet
25	46	25. Innocence (The Unexpected)	46. Pushing Upward
26	45	26. The Taming Power of the Great	45. Gathering Together [Massing]
Line Opposite Pairs No K'un, Ch'ien			
17	18	17. Following	18. Work on what has been Spoiled [Decay]
3 (19)	50	3.(19) Difficulty at the Beginning	50. The Caldron
4 (20)	49	4. (20) Youthful Folly	49. Revolution (Molting)
21	48	21. Biting Through	48. The Well
22	47	22. Grace	47. Oppression (Exhaustion)
27	28	27. Corners of the Mouth (Providing Nourishment)	28. Preponderance of the Great
29	30	29. K'an / The Abysmal (Water)	30. Li / The Clinging, Fire
31	41	31. Influence (Wooing)	41. Decrease
32	42	32. Duration	42. Increase
37	40	37. The Family [The Clan]	40. Deliverance
38	39	38. Opposition	39. Obstruction
51	57	51. Chên / The Arousing (Shock, Thunder)	57. Sun / The Gentle (The Penetrating, Wind)
52	58	52. Kên / Keeping Still, Mountain	58. Tui / The Joyous, Lake
53	54	53. Development (Gradual Progress)	54. The Marrying Maiden
55	59	55. Abundance [Fullness]	59. Dispersion [Dissolution]
56	60	56. The Wanderer	60. Limitation
61	62	61. Inner Truth	62. Preponderance of the Small
63	64	63. After Completion	64. Before Completion

One interesting feature of King Wen's puzzle is that he switched the 3, 4 and the 19, 20 hexagram pairs. It certainly proved to be a highly effective spoiler. I believe he made this adjustment after completing the numerical order. The titles of hexagrams 3, Difficulty at the Beginning, and 4, Youthful Folly, are especially telling. In my opinion, it seems clear that he followed the following process.

First, he assembled all line-to-line opposite hexagrams.
Second, he split out the twenty-eight hexagrams with a triple broken-line or triple solid-line trigram.
Third, he assembled all the two-pair sets with their flip pairs. This created groups of four.

Fourth, he realized the Primary and Complimentary hexagrams do not have flip pairs, but they do form sets of eight hexagrams according to their own rules or processes.

Fifth, he realized he could form three houses of eight hexagrams each using only hexagrams with a triple broken-line or a triple solid-line trigram. Now he had six houses with eight hexagrams in each. The Primary and the Complimentary houses each had a pair of with the Yin/Yang trigram configuration for a total of 8x3=24+2+2=28

Sixth, he wrote the oracle as house groups, especially focusing on the sets of four.

Seventh, he numbered his arrangement so that his method was not entirely lost yet spread out in a way that would be difficult to decode.

Eighth, he realized that he needed to plant additional confusion about his method, so he switched the 19 and 20 into the 3 and 4 positions.

King Wen Houses- Each row = 1 house; Wilhelm/Baynes titles

1 — Creative — 63	2 — Receptive — 0	27 — Corners of the Mouth — 33	28 — Preponderance of the Great — 30	29 — The Abysmal Water — 18	30 — The Clinging Fire — 45	61 — Inner Truth — 51	62 — Preponderance of the Small — 12
19 (3) — Approach — 3	20 (4) — Contemplation — 48	33 — Retreat — 60	34 — Power of the Great — 15	5 — Waiting Nourishment — 23	6 — Conflict — 58	35 — Progress — 40	36 — Darkening of the Light — 5
7 — The Army — 2	8 — Holding Together Union — 16	13 — Fellowship with Men — 61	14 — Possession in Great Measure — 47	9 — Taming Power of the Small — 55	10 — Treading Conduct — 59	15 — Modesty — 4	16 — Enthusiasm — 8
23 — Splitting Apart — 32	24 — Return The Turning Point — 1	43 — Breakthrough Resoluteness — 31	44 — Coming to Meet — 62	25 — Innocence — 57	26 — Taming Power of the Great — 39	45 — Pushing Upwards — 24	46 — Gathering Together — 6
3 (19) — Difficulty at the Beginning — 17	4 (20) — Youthful Folly — 34	49 — Revolution Molting — 29	50 — The Cauldron — 46	21 — Biting Through — 41	22 — Grace — 37	47 — Oppression Exhaustion — 26	48 — The Well — 22
31 — Influence Wooing — 28	32 — Duration — 14	41 — Decrease — 35	42 — Increase — 49	37 — The Family — 53	38 — Opposition — 43	39 — Obstruction — 20	40 — Deliverance — 10
51 — The Arousing Shock, Thunder — 9	52 — Keeping Still Mountain — 36	57 — The Gentle Penetrating Wind — 54	58 — The Joyous Lake — 27	55 — Abundance Fullness — 13	56 — The Wanderer — 44	59 — Dispersion Dissolution — 50	60 — Limitation — 19
11 — Peace — 7	12 — Standstill Stagnation — 56	17 — Following — 25	18 — Work on What Has Been Spoiled — 38	53 — Development Gradual Progress — 52	54 — The Marrying Maiden — 11	63 — After Completion — 21	64 — Before Completion — 42

4: House Charts, Geometry, and Magic Squares

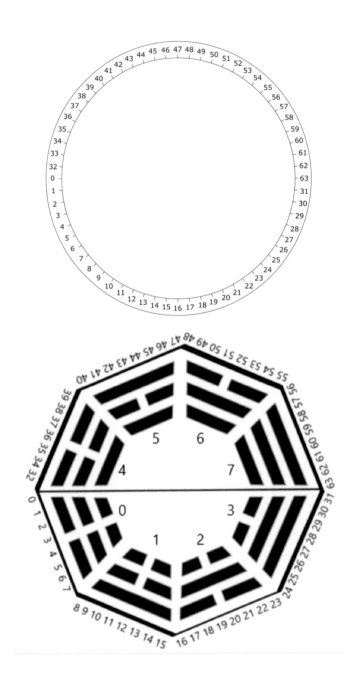

Soon after discovering the house groups, I created a simple version of the hexagram wheel and plotted the houses into geometric patterns as shown below.

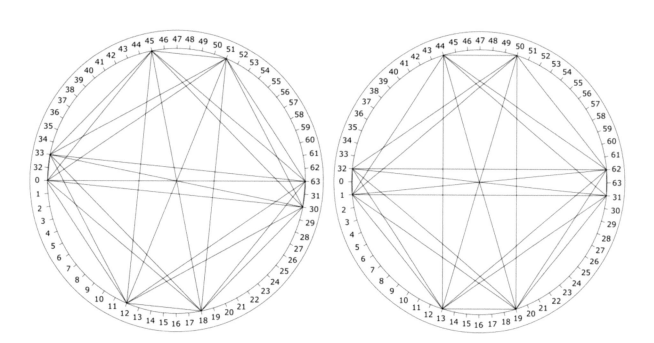
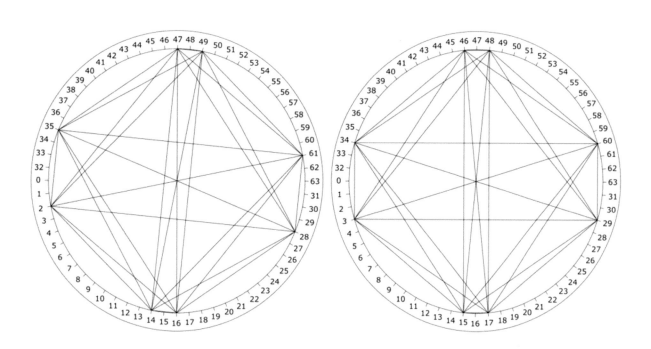

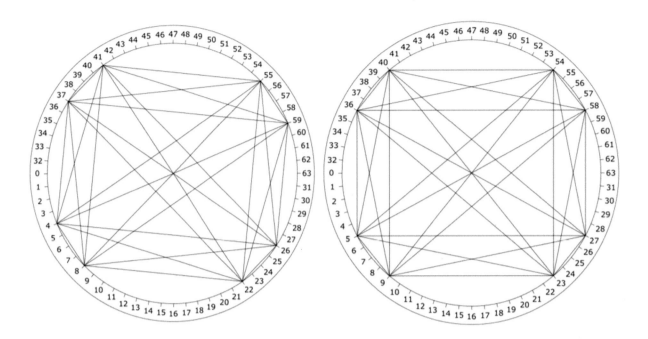

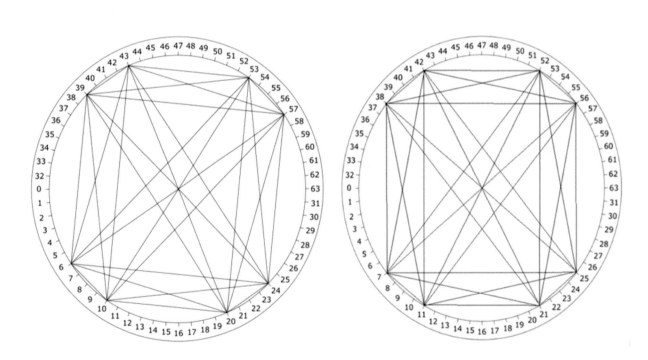

After assembling the house charts, it was clear that locked inside the binary numbers of *I Ching* was a code for an ancient form of geometry. The geometric angles used today are based on segments of a 360-degree circle. The angles of the Earlier Heaven trigram wheel are based on segments of a 64-degree circle. By dividing 360 by 64 we can compare the modern system of angles to the ancient one. Each of the 64 degrees in the Earlier Heaven sequence is equal to 5.625 degrees of our present measurement system.

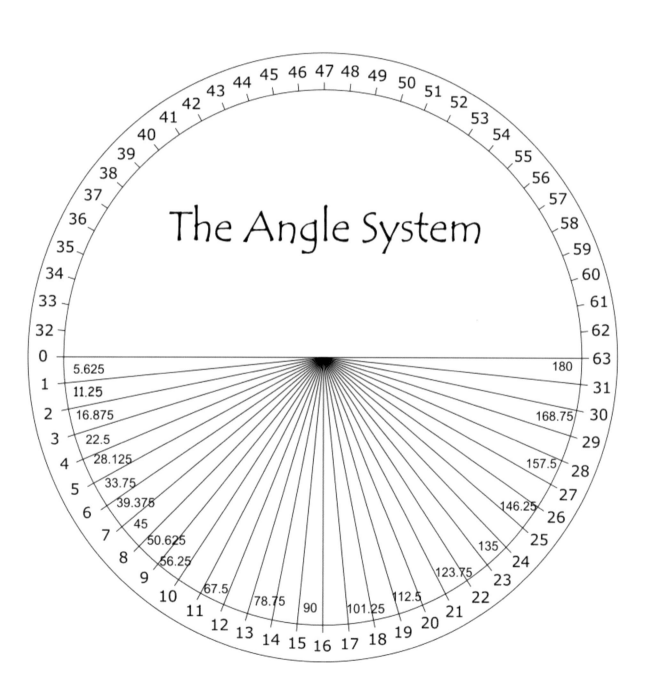

The Angle System

Combined houses also generate interesting geometric patterns.

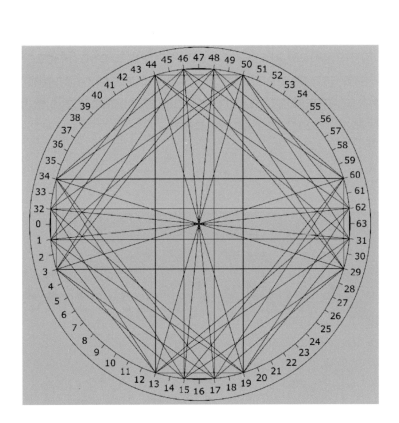

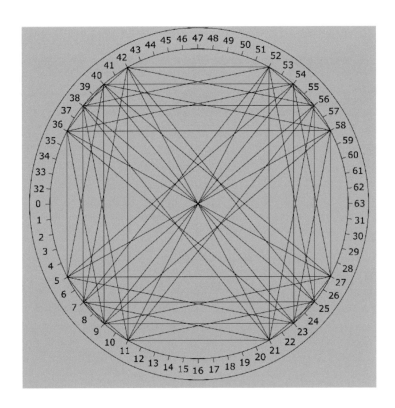

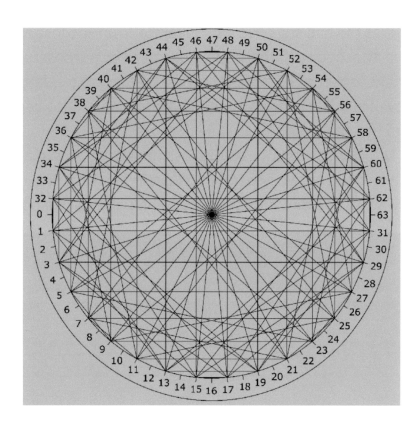

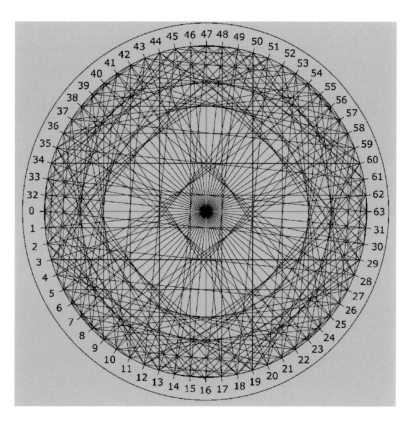

The Earlier Heaven trigram wheel encodes a split binary system. The more deeply I studied it as the ancient code it is, separate from the fascinating myth and magic which have attached to it, the more I recognize its purposeful binary logic. The most important aspect of its directionality is that it also displays duality. The lower values move from left to right while the higher values also begin on the left and move toward the right.

The 1703 Leibnitz document also displays the hexagrams in a split binary order in which they move as two separate and distinct halves. This causes the hexagrams to always reside directly across from their line-to-line opposites.

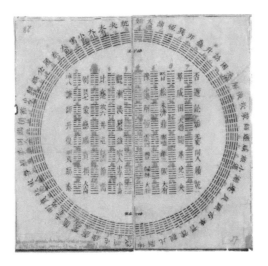

With this split system in mind, there is a fascinating artifact called the Narmer Palette, housed in the Egyptian Museum in Cairo. It is a two-sided carved stone plate which has been reliably dated at 3200 to 3000 BC. When I saw it in a photograph, I instantly recognized the split circle created by the long-necked beasts. Are these two ancient artifacts related? Do they have shared roots in an even earlier culture and long forgotten system of knowledge?

Finding Magic Squares

In a college art history class long ago, I had learned about the 1514 engraving by Albrecht Durer called Melencolia 1. At the time, I felt an instant affinity for the determined angel, lost in contemplation of things she might never comprehend. When I came upon a picture of her on the Internet, the accompanying article turned out to be about magic squares.

Although I had never thought much about them, I read on. It turns out that above the angel's wings, Durer included a magic square. This one has numbers which always add up to 34 whether they are combined in rows, columns, or diagonals. Other famous thinkers were also enamored of figuring out possible magic square solutions. Benjamin Franklin, for example, spent a lot of time and paper in his search for magic squares, and some of the results of his toil can be found in his writings.

Soon after assembling the binary house chart, I realized the hexagrams within each house act as four binary pairs. Binary pairs necessarily add up to sixty-three because they are line-to-line opposites. Together, each line position is represented once as a solid line and once as a broken line. Therefore, each binary pair can be thought of as one complete hexagram of solid lines which totals seven for the lower trigram plus fifty-six
for the upper trigram These two fully "on" trigrams total sixty-three. Taking this a step further mathematically, four pairs per house times sixty-three equals two hundred fifty-two, or 4 x 63 = 252.

I awoke the morning after reading the Melencolia article convinced that the houses could be arranged into a magic square. As it turned out, this was a correct assumption. Leaving the hexagrams in family groups and in their original rows, I arranged them into sequential order from least to greatest. I knew the target total for the columns and the diagonals was 252. I first created the following chart.

0	12	18	30	33	45	51	63
1	13	19	31	32	44	50	62
2	14	16	28	35	47	49	61
3	15	17	29	34	46	48	60
4	8	22	26	37	41	55	59
5	9	23	27	36	40	54	58
6	10	20	24	39	43	53	57
7	11	21	25	38	42	52	56

I could see I would need to reverse half the rows to achieve numerical symmetry within columns. First, I tried switching every other row, but that did not work. After a few calculations and a couple more tries, I found the solution below.

It was almost too easy. All rows, columns and diagonals added up to 252. This diagram is the resulting Magic Square.

0	12	18	30	33	45	51	63
1	13	19	31	32	44	50	62
61	49	47	35	28	16	14	2
60	48	46	34	29	17	15	3
59	55	41	37	26	22	8	4
58	54	40	36	27	23	9	5
6	10	20	24	39	43	53	57
7	11	21	25	38	42	52	56

Eventually, I found this second magic square.

0	14	18	28	33	47	51	61
1	15	19	29	32	46	50	60
63	49	45	35	30	16	12	2
62	48	44	34	31	17	13	3
57	55	43	37	24	22	10	4
56	54	42	36	25	23	11	5
6	8	20	26	39	41	53	59
7	9	21	27	38	40	52	58

Magic Square

5: Pyramids

What if I told you the code for blueprints of ancient pyramids has been hiding in plain sight for at least 3000 years? There are numerous unsolved mysteries surrounding ancient pyramids. Who built them? Exactly when were they built? How were our ancestors able to accomplish the construction of these huge structures? What was their original envisioned use? When and how did the basics of pyramid design travel to the new world? What caused the design to go out of fashion, so to speak? All these are fascinating riddles which continue to inspire serious research, intelligent speculation, and outright fantasy. Like the proverbial elephant in the room, there is one obvious question which generally gets left out of the conversation. Why did the ancients build pyramids in the first place?

I used to wonder if ancient people decided to build pyramids to replicate distant mountain peaks. It is a thought, but pyramids are distinctly not mountains.

They are a regular solid shape, based on mathematically calculated angles. They are finely planned and executed geometric structures touting design and engineering expertise. We cannot help but be amazed at their architectural brilliance. If past cultures wanted to build mountains, they could have far more simply piled up rock, clay, and dirt into interesting abstract forms. So, if they were not attempting to mimic mountains, what did inspire the ancients to design and construct these megalithic pyramidal structures?

In 2020, I discovered a possible answer that had been hidden in plain sight for millennia. When I began my research, I was not looking for any type of mathematics, nor was I thinking of pyramids in the slightest. Even after the information had fully unveiled itself, I was still hesitant to believe what I had found. Had a blueprint for four-sided pyramids been hiding within the pages of a long-standing, tediously studied, ancient Chinese text? Who would have thought to seek answers concerning Egyptian pyramids within the *Book of Changes*, or *I Ching*, as it is known in the western world? I was astounded. As it turns out, the geometry of ancient pyramids has been preserved as a binary code unwittingly disguised as an oracle for millennia.

Since youth, I have been fascinated by ancient history and our wide world of cultures. In 1968, Erich Anton Paul von Däniken wrote his best-selling book, Chariots of the Gods. I was an impressionable eleven-year-old. Reading it, and later watching the documentary, I was far more interested in the ancient sites, artifacts, and architecture it brought into my awareness than the notion of any alien assistance in constructing these wonders. From that time forward, I became a seeker after the truth of human culture and change. In this endeavor, I have searched through and studied historical, artistic, geologic, occult, and religious accounts of the human timeline. Human innovation and creativity have remained fascinating to me.

During my early observations of the initial eight house maps, some things were obvious, and some things were more hidden. It did not take a great imagination, however, to realize that pyramid models played a central role in the geometry of this system. The first two house images in the odd and even sets, 0 and 2, and 1 and 3, feature double pyramids with similar angles to "The Great Pyramid of Giza" pointing in east/west and north/south directions. The angles of the faces are 50.625 degrees at the two bases and 78.75 degrees at the apex.

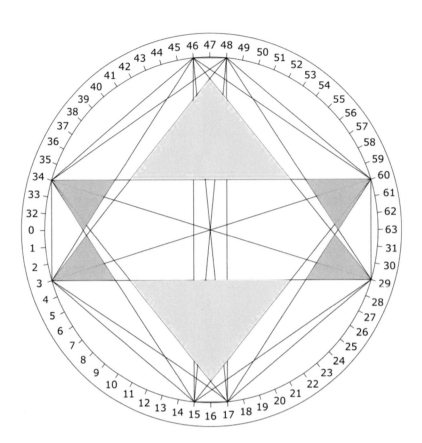

The next diagram shows how the angles of this pyramid are calculated using the 64-point system.

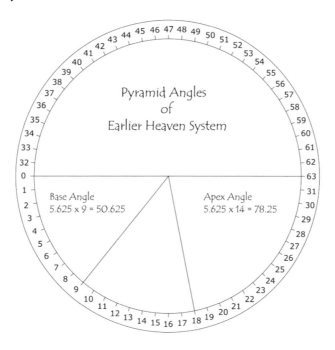

The next diagram shows the four apexes of the 14-point (78.75 degree) pyramid shaded in grey and the eight base points shaded in green. The inner square which connects the apexes has the same area as the circle. The outer square connects the bases.

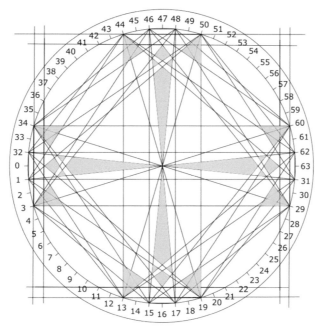

Ancient pyramids have survived into our modern times and continue to exist in various locations including China, South and Central America, Mexico, and Egypt. They have been measured and scrutinized, calculated, debated, and highly publicized. Does this ancient geometric system from deep in Chinese prehistory have a direct connection to these structures? After uncovering and studying this lost system of mathematical knowledge, one thing is clear to me; the Earlier Heaven trigram code existed as a potential
blueprint for pyramidal structures long before it was changed into an oracle.

The next picture shows a model I built using four charts of all houses mapped together. Notice the interconnected, puzzle-like structure of the diagrams. They seem instructive, like blueprints.

There are four pyramid types which can be modeled by cutting out them out of the circle along their four base lines, and then folding and pinching them into the center to join the bases. The next picture shows how these four pyramids compare to each other in terms of height and angles.

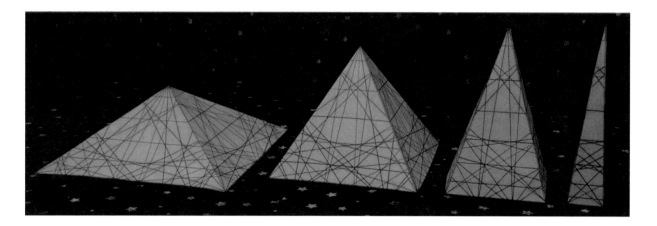

4 Central Pyramids (even group)			
2 Point or 11.25 degrees	6 Point or 33.75 degrees	10 Point or 56.25 degrees	14 Point or 78.75 degrees
0-33 yellow	2-35 blue	4-37 red	6-39 orange
14-16 blue	12-18 yellow	10-20 orange	8-22 red
30-63 yellow	28-61 blue	26-59 red	24-57 orange
47-49 blue	45-51 yellow	43-53 orange	41-55 red
Yellow and Blue House Pyramids		Red and Orange House Pyramids	

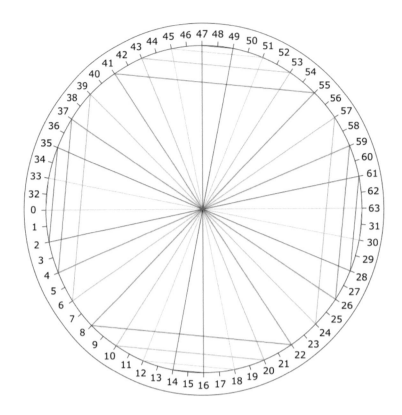

Although there are four pyramids with four differing apex angles which can be modeled from the center point, the 14-point apex pyramid is clearly highlighted. It is distinctly depicted in various sizes.

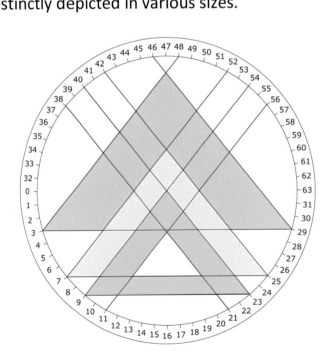

The Great Pyramid of Giza

When I first realized the geometry inherent in the 64 hexagrams produced a diagram for a four-sided pyramid, I immediately wondered if the angle measurements would match up to the Great Pyramid of Giza. Although close, they were not the exact measurements. The accepted Great Pyramid base angles are 51.84 degrees which produces apex angles of 76.32 degrees. The base angles of the pyramid coded in the Earlier Heaven trigram wheel are 50.625, and the apex is 78.25 degrees. I therefore assumed, since the I Ching is so strongly connected to ancient China, that the Egyptians might have been working from a different measurement system. Still, as I researched various documentaries featuring Sumerian texts and artifacts, I kept noticing eight-sided images depicting objects such as suns or flowers. Additionally, I knew that Indian mandala art is built on octagonal shapes. I started to wonder if ancient cultures from the Nile to the Yellow River were all using a similar ancient geometry built on a 64-degree system.

The next picture is of a lotus tile in the Badami Cave Temples in India. The tic marks around the outside circle total 64 when the petal edges are counted. The next row of petals numbers 16 and divides the outer lines into equal sections of four.

As I continued to study the many ancient artifacts depicting circles divided into eight main parts, I decided to look for the Great Pyramid angles within the house systems I had identified. My effort was successful with a far easier solution than I had expected. The first diagram below shows exactly where the angles of the Great Pyramid are located and how they align with the more explicitly featured pyramid of the house systems. The red lines represent the north pointing face of the Giza Pyramid. Notice that the apex point aligns with the octagonal division, shown in blue, within the greater circle. The bases utilize the same points as those of the inherent system pyramid. The pyramid peaks at the central conjunction created (at the top) by the 34, 48 and 60, 46, point connections. Clearly, these points are not randomly placed.

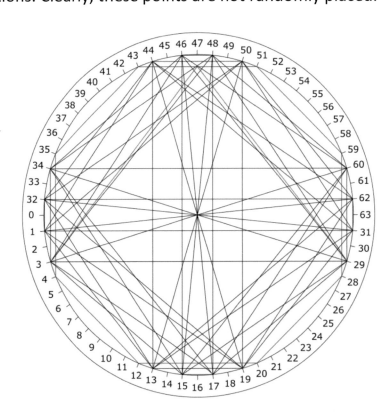

For the next diagram, I removed excess lines so that it is easier to see exactly where the Great Pyramid angle system is located. The blue lines depict the octagon which the four apex points of the pyramid connect to at the north/south, east/west centers. The green lines show how the base lines are aligned to a six-point, ten-point configuration. The geometry of the Great Pyramid works perfectly within the 64-degree system.

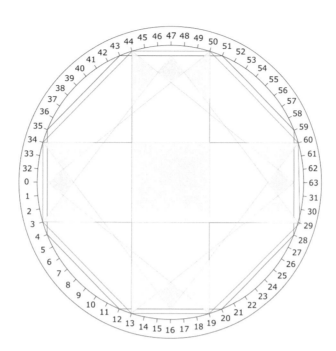

The following is a picture of a model I built using the diagram of the Great Pyramid as described. Notice that the Giza pyramid model creates a circle and square image around the apex of the pyramid.

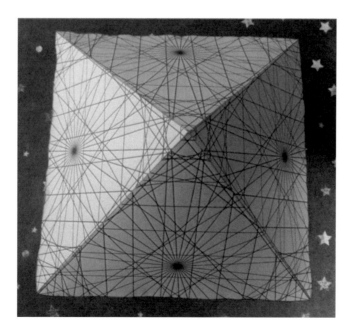

The picture below is of two copper models I built to compare the size of the Earlier Heaven pyramid to the adjusted Giza pyramid. They have the same base length. The taller pyramid on the right is the Giza model.

6: Conclusions

It turns out life is a biotechnological, mathematical, event-steered, interconnected structure. We know life exists here on planet Earth. Does it exist on other planets, on their moons, in other solar systems and galaxies? Probably, but for now we can only guess. The life we can experience, examine, observe, and appreciate is surrounding us right here on this one elemental speck in an unfathomable universe. This is our own planetary life of which we are an integral part. How did life start? How did it change and progress to become what it is today?

Earthly life is built from two distinct systems, which, when brought together, can begin to produce a diffusion of life forms. As a direct result of their presence, these various life forms help orchestrate new life supportive alterations to the original elemental platform. Soil, air composition, a plethora of food sources create are the result of life forms and constantly bring forth new platforms and niches for species building.

The first necessary component for life as found on this planet is the system of elements. Generally, young people begin to learn about elements in school by looking at a periodic table. This table identifies the atomic compositions of the basic ingredients from which our three-dimensional world is composed. The chart begins with the lightest elements, Helium and Hydrogen, and moves on to heavier and more atomically complex forms.

The second system required for Earthly life is the DNA code. The DNA code is a binary, 64-bit, biotechnological, mathematical code which relies upon its own growth-adaptive potentials as it effectively and efficiently utilizes the elemental components at hand. The DNA code is a binary mathematical language built on four distinct codon types combined into all possible sets of three. These 64 sets of three codons each result in amino acids. The human body uses 21 amino acids to create all the proteins it requires to compose itself, function and grow.

Considering the above, life on this planet can be categorized as Elemental/Complex. Life is elemental because it exists within, is built upon, and is limited by a specific set of three-dimensional atomic structures. Life is complex because it is built upon a 64-bit, binary DNA code which can assemble a vast possibility of seemingly distinct life forms. These forms, or life-events, can range from the simplest single-cell plants and animals to plants and animals in their presently most complex arrangements.

One might look at this waltz of life across Earth as the hand of God. One might perceive only a scientific led event. However you view this complexity of interdependent life, each divergent form built from and carrying the same 64-bit code, I hope you will think long and hard on attempting alterations to the structure. No human has the foresight or right to manipulate the code of life. Please tread lightly.

7: Unique Position Sets

Column 0, 1st Row

000 P-0 0 GLY	001 P-68 1 GLY	002 P-93 2 GLY	003 P-7 3 GLY
020 P-12 8 VAL	021 P-42 9 VAL	022 P-45 10 VAL	023 P-11 11 VAL
100 P-51 16 ARG	101 P-21 17 ARG	102 P-18 18 SER	103 P-52 19 SER
120 P-63 24 MET	121 P-25 25 ILE	122 P-90 26 ILE	123 P-56 27 ILE

Column 4, 5th Row

210 P-7 36 STOP	211 P-93 37 STOP	212 P-68 38 TYR	213 P-0 39 TYR
230 P-11 44 SER	231 P-45 45 SER	232 P-42 46 SER	233 P-12 47 SER
310 P-52 52 GLN	311 P-18 53 GLN	312 P-21 54 HIS	313 P-51 55 HIS
330 P-56 60 PRO	331 P-90 61 PRO	332 P-25 62 PRO	333 P-63 63 PRO

Column 0, 2nd Row

020 P-12	021 P-42	022 P-45	023 P-11
8 VAL	9 VAL	10 VAL	11 VAL
100 P-51	101 P-21	102 P-18	103 P-52
16 ARG	17 ARG	18 SER	19 SER
120 P-63	121 P-25	122 P-80	123 P-56
24 MET	25 ILE	26 ILE	27 ILE
200 P-7	201 P-33	202 P-38	203 P-0
32 TRP	33 STOP	34 CYS	35 CYS

Column 4, 4th Row

130 P-63	131 P-25	132 P-80	133 P-56
28 THR	29 THR	30 THR	31 THR
210 P-7	211 P-33	212 P-38	213 P-0
36 STOP	37 STOP	38 TYR	39 TYR
230 P-11	231 P-45	232 P-42	233 P-12
44 SER	45 SER	46 SER	47 SER
310 P-52	311 P-18	312 P-21	313 P-51
52 GLN	53 GLN	54 HIS	55 HIS

Column 0, 3rd Row

100 P-51	101 P-21	102 P-18	103 P-52
16 ARG	17 ARG	18 SER	19 SER
120 P-63	121 P-25	122 P-30	123 P-56
24 MET	25 ILE	26 ILE	27 ILE
200 P-7	201 P-33	202 P-38	203 P-0
32 TRP	33 STOP	34 CYS	35 CYS
220 P-11	221 P-45	222 P-42	223 P-12
40 LEU	41 LEU	42 PHE	43 PHE

Column 4, 3rd Row

110 P-51	111 P-21	112 P-18	113 P-52
20 LYS	21 LYS	22 ASN	23 ASN
130 P-63	131 P-25	132 P-30	133 P-56
28 THR	29 THR	30 THR	31 THR
210 P-7	211 P-63	212 P-38	213 P-0
36 STOP	37 STOP	38 TYR	39 TYR
230 P-11	231 P-45	232 P-42	233 P-12
44 SER	45 SER	46 SER	47 SER

Column 0, 4th Row

120 P-63	121 P-25	122 P-30	123 P-56
24 MET	25 ILE	26 ILE	27 ILE
200 P-7	201 P-33	202 P-38	203 P-0
32 TRP	33 STOP	34 CYS	35 CYS
220 P-11	221 P-45	222 P-42	223 P-12
40 LEU	41 LEU	42 PHE	43 PHE
300 P-52	301 P-18	302 P-21	303 P-51
48 ARG	49 ARG	50 ARG	51 ARG

Column 4, 2nd Row

030 P-12	031 P-42	032 P-45	033 P-11
12 ALA	13 ALA	14 ALA	15 ALA
110 P-51	111 P-21	112 P-18	113 P-52
20 LYS	21 LYS	22 ASN	23 ASN
130 P-63	131 P-25	132 P-30	133 P-56
28 THR	29 THR	30 THR	31 THR
210 P-7	211 P-33	212 P-38	213 P-0
36 STOP	37 STOP	38 TYR	39 TYR

Column 0, 5th Row

	200 P-7		201 P-33		202 P-58		203 P-0
	32 TRP		33 STOP		34 CYS		35 CYS
	220 P-11		221 P-45		222 P-42		223 P-12
	40 LEU		41 LEU		42 PHE		43 PHE
	300 P-52		301 P-18		302 P-21		303 P-51
	48 ARG		49 ARG		50 ARG		51 ARG
	320 P-56		321 P-30		322 P-25		323 P-63
	56 LEU		57 LEU		58 LEU		59 LEU

Column 4, 1st Row

	010 P-0		011 P-58		012 P-33		013 P-7
	4 GLU		5 GLU		6 ASP		7 ASP
	030 P-12		031 P-42		032 P-45		033 P-11
	12 ALA		13 ALA		14 ALA		15 ALA
	110 P-51		111 P-21		112 P-18		113 P-52
	20 LYS		21 LYS		22 ASN		23 ASN
	130 P-63		131 P-25		132 P-30		133 P-56
	28 THR		29 THR		30 THR		31 THR

Column 0, 6th Row

220 P-11 · 40 LEU	221 P-45 · 41 LEU	222 P-42 · 42 PHE	223 P-12 · 43 PHE
300 P-52 · 48 ARG	301 P-18 · 49 ARG	302 P-21 · 50 ARG	303 P-51 · 51 ARG
320 P-56 · 56 LEU	321 P-30 · 57 LEU	322 P-25 · 58 LEU	323 P-63 · 59 LEU
000 P-0 · 0 GLY	001 P-38 · 1 GLY	002 P-33 · 2 GLY	003 P-7 · 3 GLY

Column 4, 8th Row

330 P-56 · 60 PRO	331 P-30 · 61 PRO	332 P-25 · 62 PRO	333 P-63 · 63 PRO
010 P-0 · 4 GLU	011 P-38 · 5 GLU	012 P-33 · 6 ASP	013 P-7 · 7 ASP
030 P-12 · 12 ALA	031 P-42 · 13 ALA	032 P-45 · 14 ALA	033 P-11 · 15 ALA
110 P-51 · 20 LYS	111 P-21 · 21 LYS	112 P-18 · 22 ASN	113 P-52 · 23 ASN

Column 0, 7th Row

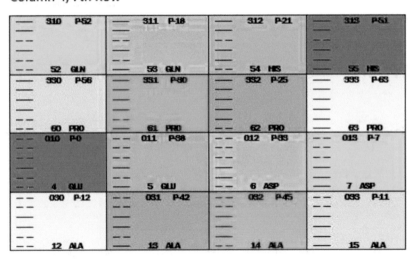

300 P-52	301 P-18	302 P-21	303 P-51
48 ARG	49 ARG	50 ARG	51 ARG
320 P-56	321 P-30	322 P-25	323 P-63
56 LEU	57 LEU	58 LEU	59 LEU
000 P-0	001 P-68	002 P-33	003 P-7
0 GLY	1 GLY	2 GLY	3 GLY
020 P-12	021 P-42	022 P-45	023 P-11
8 VAL	9 VAL	10 VAL	11 VAL

Column 4, 7th Row

310 P-52	311 P-18	312 P-21	313 P-51
52 GLN	53 GLN	54 HIS	55 HIS
330 P-56	331 P-30	332 P-25	333 P-63
60 PRO	61 PRO	62 PRO	63 PRO
010 P-0	011 P-38	012 P-33	013 P-7
4 GLU	5 GLU	6 ASP	7 ASP
030 P-12	031 P-42	032 P-45	033 P-11
12 ALA	13 ALA	14 ALA	15 ALA

Column 0, 8th Row

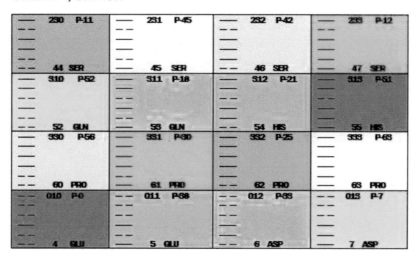

320 P-56	321 P-30	322 P-25	323 P-65
56 LEU	57 LEU	58 LEU	59 LEU
000 P-0	001 P-38	002 P-33	003 P-7
0 GLY	1 GLY	2 GLY	3 GLY
020 P-12	021 P-42	022 P-45	023 P-11
8 VAL	9 VAL	10 VAL	11 VAL
100 P-51	101 P-21	102 P-18	103 P-52
16 ARG	17 ARG	18 SER	19 SER

Column 4, 6th Row

230 P-11	231 P-45	232 P-42	233 P-12
44 SER	45 SER	46 SER	47 SER
310 P-52	311 P-18	312 P-21	313 P-51
52 GLN	53 GLN	54 HIS	55 HIS
330 P-56	331 P-30	332 P-25	333 P-63
60 PRO	61 PRO	62 PRO	63 PRO
010 P-0	011 P-38	012 P-33	013 P-7
4 GLU	5 GLU	6 ASP	7 ASP

Column 1, 1st Row

001 P-38	002 P-33	003 P-7	010 P-0
1 GLY	2 GLY	3 GLY	4 GLU
021 P-42	022 P-45	023 P-11	030 P-12
9 VAL	10 VAL	11 VAL	12 ALA
101 P-21	102 P-18	103 P-52	110 P-51
17 ARG	18 SER	19 SER	20 LYS
121 P-25	122 P-90	123 P-56	130 P-63
25 ILE	26 ILE	27 ILE	28 THR

Column 3, 5th Row

203 P-0	210 P-7	211 P-33	212 P-38
35 CYS	36 STOP	37 STOP	38 TYR
223 P-12	230 P-11	231 P-45	232 P-42
43 PHE	44 SER	45 SER	46 SER
303 P-51	310 P-52	311 P-18	312 P-21
51 ARG	52 GLN	53 GLN	54 HIS
323 P-63	330 P-56	331 P-90	332 P-25
59 LEU	60 PRO	61 PRO	62 PRO

Column 1, 2nd Row

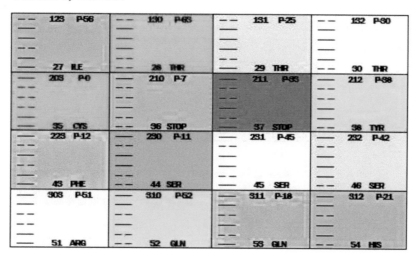

021 P-42	022 P-45	023 P-11	030 P-12
9 VAL	10 VAL	11 VAL	12 ALA
101 P-21	102 P-18	103 P-52	110 P-51
17 ARG	18 SER	19 SER	20 LYS
121 P-25	122 P-80	123 P-56	130 P-65
25 ILE	26 ILE	27 ILE	28 THR
201 P-65	202 P-98	203 P-0	210 P-7
33 STOP	34 CYS	35 CYS	36 STOP

Column 3, 4th Row

123 P-56	130 P-65	131 P-25	132 P-80
27 ILE	28 THR	29 THR	30 THR
203 P-0	210 P-7	211 P-65	212 P-98
35 CYS	36 STOP	37 STOP	38 TYR
223 P-12	230 P-11	231 P-45	232 P-42
43 PHE	44 SER	45 SER	46 SER
303 P-51	310 P-52	311 P-18	312 P-21
51 ARG	52 GLN	53 GLN	54 HIS

Column 1, 3rd Row

101 P-21	102 P-18	103 P-52	110 P-51
17 ARG	18 SER	19 SER	20 LYS
121 P-25	122 P-80	123 P-56	130 P-63
25 ILE	26 ILE	27 ILE	28 THR
201 P-33	202 P-38	203 P-0	210 P-7
33 STOP	34 CYS	35 CYS	36 STOP
221 P-45	222 P-42	223 P-12	230 P-11
41 LEU	42 PHE	43 PHE	44 SER

Column 3, 3rd Row

103 P-52	110 P-51	111 P-21	112 P-18
19 SER	20 LYS	21 LYS	22 ASN
123 P-56	130 P-63	131 P-25	132 P-80
27 ILE	28 THR	29 THR	30 THR
203 P-0	210 P-7	211 P-33	212 P-38
35 CYS	36 STOP	37 STOP	38 TYR
223 P-12	230 P-11	231 P-45	232 P-42
43 PHE	44 SER	45 SER	46 SER

Column 1, 4th Row

121 P-25	122 P-90	123 P-56	130 P-63
25 ILE	26 ILE	27 ILE	28 THR
201 P-63	202 P-38	203 P-0	210 P-7
33 STOP	34 CYS	35 CYS	36 STOP
221 P-45	222 P-42	223 P-12	230 P-11
41 LEU	42 PHE	43 PHE	44 SER
301 P-18	302 P-21	303 P-51	310 P-52
49 ARG	50 ARG	51 ARG	52 GLN

Column 3, 2nd Row

029 P-11	030 P-12	031 P-42	032 P-45
11 VAL	12 ALA	13 ALA	14 ALA
109 P-52	110 P-51	111 P-21	112 P-18
19 SER	20 LYS	21 LYS	22 ASN
129 P-56	130 P-63	131 P-25	132 P-90
27 ILE	28 THR	29 THR	30 THR
209 P-0	210 P-7	211 P-63	212 P-38
35 CYS	36 STOP	37 STOP	38 TYR

Column 1, 5th Row

201 P-33	202 P-38	203 P-0	210 P-7
33 STOP	34 CYS	35 CYS	36 STOP
221 P-45	222 P-42	223 P-12	230 P-11
41 LEU	42 PHE	43 PHE	44 SER
301 P-18	302 P-21	303 P-51	310 P-52
49 ARG	50 ARG	51 ARG	52 GLN
321 P-30	322 P-25	323 P-63	330 P-56
57 LEU	58 LEU	59 LEU	60 PRO

Column 3, 1st Row

003 P-7	010 P-0	011 P-38	012 P-33
3 GLY	4 GLU	5 GLU	6 ASP
023 P-11	030 P-12	031 P-42	032 P-45
11 VAL	12 ALA	13 ALA	14 ALA
103 P-52	110 P-51	111 P-21	112 P-18
19 SER	20 LYS	21 LYS	22 ASN
123 P-56	130 P-63	131 P-25	132 P-30
27 ILE	28 THR	29 THR	30 THR

Column 1, 6th Row

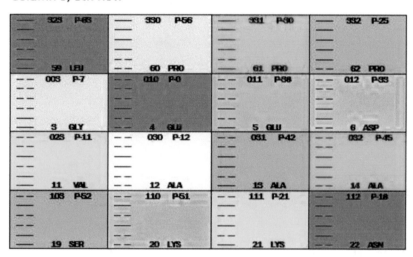

Column 3, 8th Row

Column 1, 7th Row

301 P-18	302 P-21	303 P-51	310 P-52
49 ARG	50 ARG	51 ARG	52 GLN
321 P-30	322 P-25	323 P-63	330 P-56
57 LEU	58 LEU	59 LEU	60 PRO
001 P-68	002 P-63	003 P-7	010 P-0
1 GLY	2 GLY	3 GLY	4 GLU
021 P-42	022 P-45	023 P-11	030 P-12
9 VAL	10 VAL	11 VAL	12 ALA

Column 3, 7th Row

303 P-51	310 P-52	311 P-18	312 P-21
51 ARG	52 GLN	53 GLN	54 HIS
323 P-63	330 P-56	331 P-30	332 P-25
59 LEU	60 PRO	61 PRO	62 PRO
003 P-7	010 P-0	011 P-68	012 P-63
3 GLY	4 GLU	5 GLU	6 ASP
023 P-11	030 P-12	031 P-42	032 P-45
11 VAL	12 ALA	13 ALA	14 ALA

Column 1, 8th Row

321 P-30		322 P-25		329 P-68		330 P-56	
57 LEU		58 LEU		59 LEU		60 PRO	
001 P-38		002 P-93		003 P-7		010 P-0	
1 GLY		2 GLY		3 GLY		4 GLU	
021 P-42		022 P-45		023 P-11		030 P-12	
9 VAL		10 VAL		11 VAL		12 ALA	
101 P-21		102 P-18		103 P-52		110 P-51	
17 ARG		18 SER		19 SER		20 LYS	

Column 3, 6th Row

229 P-12		230 P-11		231 P-45		232 P-42	
43 PHE		44 SER		45 SER		46 SER	
309 P-51		310 P-52		311 P-18		312 P-21	
51 ARG		52 GLN		53 GLN		54 HIS	
329 P-68		330 P-56		331 P-30		332 P-25	
59 LEU		60 PRO		61 PRO		62 PRO	
003 P-7		010 P-0		011 P-38		012 P-93	
3 GLY		4 GLU		5 GLU		6 ASP	

Column 2, 1st Row

002 P-35		003 P-7		010 P-0		011 P-38	
2 GLY		3 GLY		4 GLU		5 GLU	
022 P-45		023 P-11		030 P-12		031 P-42	
10 VAL		11 VAL		12 ALA		13 ALA	
102 P-18		103 P-52		110 P-51		111 P-21	
18 SER		19 SER		20 LYS		21 LYS	
122 P-30		123 P-56		130 P-65		131 P-25	
26 ILE		27 ILE		28 THR		29 THR	

Column 2, 5th Row

202 P-38		203 P-0		210 P-7		211 P-35	
34 CYS		35 CYS		36 STOP		37 STOP	
222 P-42		223 P-12		230 P-11		231 P-45	
42 PHE		43 PHE		44 SER		45 SER	
302 P-21		303 P-51		310 P-52		311 P-18	
50 ARG		51 ARG		52 GLN		53 GLN	
322 P-25		323 P-65		330 P-56		331 P-30	
58 LEU		59 LEU		60 PRO		61 PRO	

Column 2, 2nd Row

022 P-45		025 P-11		030 P-12		031 P-42	
10 VAL		11 VAL		12 ALA		13 ALA	
102 P-18		103 P-52		110 P-51		111 P-21	
18 SER		19 SER		20 LYS		21 LYS	
122 P-30		123 P-56		130 P-63		131 P-25	
26 ILE		27 ILE		28 THR		29 THR	
202 P-38		203 P-0		210 P-7		211 P-33	
34 CYS		35 CYS		36 STOP		37 STOP	

Column 2, 4th Row

122 P-30		123 P-56		130 P-63		131 P-25	
26 ILE		27 ILE		28 THR		29 THR	
202 P-38		203 P-0		210 P-7		211 P-33	
34 CYS		35 CYS		36 STOP		37 STOP	
222 P-42		223 P-12		230 P-11		231 P-45	
42 PHE		43 PHE		44 SER		45 SER	
302 P-21		303 P-51		310 P-52		311 P-18	
50 ARG		51 ARG		52 GLN		53 GLN	

102 P-18	103 P-52	110 P-51	111 P-21
18 SER	19 SER	20 LYS	21 LYS
122 P-80	123 P-56	130 P-68	131 P-25
26 ILE	27 ILE	28 THR	29 THR
202 P-38	203 P-0	210 P-7	211 P-65
34 CYS	35 CYS	36 STOP	37 STOP
222 P-42	223 P-12	230 P-11	231 P-45
42 PHE	43 PHE	44 SER	45 SER

Column 2, 3rd Row

102 P-18	103 P-52	110 P-51	111 P-21
18 SER	19 SER	20 LYS	21 LYS
122 P-80	123 P-56	130 P-68	131 P-25
26 ILE	27 ILE	28 THR	29 THR
202 P-38	203 P-0	210 P-7	211 P-65
34 CYS	35 CYS	36 STOP	37 STOP
222 P-42	223 P-12	230 P-11	231 P-45
42 PHE	43 PHE	44 SER	45 SER

Column 2, 6th Row

222 P-42	223 P-12	230 P-11	231 P-45
42 PHE	43 PHE	44 SER	45 SER
302 P-21	303 P-51	310 P-52	311 P-18
50 ARG	51 ARG	52 GLN	53 GLN
322 P-25	323 P-68	330 P-56	331 P-30
58 LEU	59 LEU	60 PRO	61 PRO
002 P-65	003 P-7	010 P-0	011 P-38
2 GLY	3 GLY	4 GLU	5 GLU

Column 2, 8th Row

322 P-25	323 P-68	330 P-56	331 P-30
58 LEU	59 LEU	60 PRO	61 PRO
002 P-65	003 P-7	010 P-0	011 P-38
2 GLY	3 GLY	4 GLU	5 GLU
022 P-45	023 P-11	030 P-12	031 P-42
10 VAL	11 VAL	12 ALA	13 ALA
102 P-18	103 P-52	110 P-51	111 P-21
18 SER	19 SER	20 LYS	21 LYS

Column 2, 7th Row

302 P-21	308 P-51	310 P-52	311 P-18
50 ARG	51 ARG	52 GLN	53 GLN
322 P-25	323 P-63	330 P-56	331 P-30
58 LEU	59 LEU	60 PRO	61 PRO
002 P-33	003 P-7	010 P-0	011 P-38
2 GLY	3 GLY	4 GLU	5 GLU
022 P-45	023 P-11	030 P-12	031 P-42
10 VAL	11 VAL	12 ALA	13 ALA

Column 2, 7th Row

302 P-21	308 P-51	310 P-52	311 P-18
50 ARG	51 ARG	52 GLN	53 GLN
322 P-25	323 P-63	330 P-56	331 P-30
58 LEU	59 LEU	60 PRO	61 PRO
002 P-33	003 P-7	010 P-0	011 P-38
2 GLY	3 GLY	4 GLU	5 GLU
022 P-45	023 P-11	030 P-12	031 P-42
10 VAL	11 VAL	12 ALA	13 ALA

Column 5, 1st Row

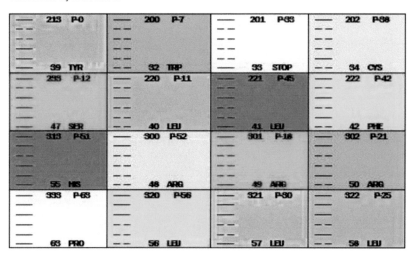

011 P-38	012 P-33	013 P-7	000 P-0
5 GLU	6 ASP	7 ASP	0 GLY
031 P-42	032 P-45	033 P-11	020 P-12
13 ALA	14 ALA	15 ALA	8 VAL
111 P-21	112 P-18	113 P-52	100 P-51
21 LYS	22 ASN	23 ASN	16 ARG
131 P-25	132 P-30	133 P-56	120 P-63
29 THR	30 THR	31 THR	24 MET

Column 7, 5th Row

213 P-0	200 P-7	201 P-33	202 P-38
39 TYR	32 TRP	33 STOP	34 CYS
233 P-12	220 P-11	221 P-45	222 P-42
47 SER	40 LEU	41 LEU	42 PHE
313 P-51	300 P-52	301 P-18	302 P-21
55 HIS	48 ARG	49 ARG	50 ARG
333 P-63	320 P-56	321 P-30	322 P-25
63 PRO	56 LEU	57 LEU	58 LEU

Column 5, 2nd Row

031 P-42 — 13 ALA	032 P-45 — 14 ALA	033 P-11 — 15 ALA	020 P-12 — 8 VAL
111 P-21 — 21 LYS	112 P-18 — 22 ASN	113 P-52 — 23 ASN	100 P-51 — 16 ARG
131 P-25 — 29 THR	132 P-30 — 30 THR	133 P-56 — 31 THR	120 P-63 — 24 MET
211 P-33 — 37 STOP	212 P-38 — 38 TYR	213 P-0 — 39 TYR	200 P-7 — 32 TRP

Column 7, 4th Row

133 P-56 — 31 THR	120 P-63 — 24 MET	121 P-25 — 25 ILE	122 P-30 — 26 ILE
213 P-0 — 39 TYR	200 P-7 — 32 TRP	201 P-33 — 33 STOP	202 P-38 — 34 CYS
233 P-12 — 47 SER	220 P-11 — 40 LEU	221 P-45 — 41 LEU	222 P-42 — 42 PHE
313 P-51 — 55 HIS	300 P-52 — 48 ARG	301 P-18 — 49 ARG	302 P-21 — 50 ARG

Column 5, 3rd Row

111 P-21	112 P-18	113 P-52	100 P-51
21 LYS	22 ASN	23 ASN	16 ARG
131 P-25	132 P-30	133 P-56	120 P-63
29 THR	30 THR	31 THR	24 MET
211 P-33	212 P-38	213 P-0	200 P-7
37 STOP	38 TYR	39 TYR	32 TRP
231 P-45	232 P-42	233 P-12	220 P-11
45 SER	46 SER	47 SER	40 LEU

Column 7, 3rd Row

113 P-52	100 P-51	101 P-21	102 P-18
23 ASN	16 ARG	17 ARG	18 SER
133 P-56	120 P-63	121 P-25	122 P-60
31 THR	24 MET	25 ILE	26 ILE
213 P-0	200 P-7	201 P-33	202 P-38
39 TYR	32 TRP	33 STOP	34 CYS
233 P-12	220 P-11	221 P-45	222 P-42
47 SER	40 LEU	41 LEU	42 PHE

Column 5, 4th Row

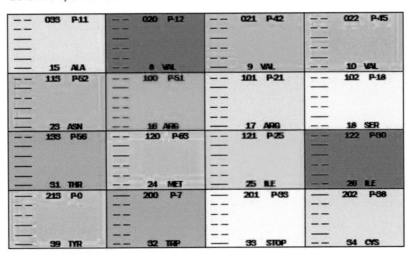

Column 7, 2nd Row

Column 5, 5th Row

211 P-33	212 P-38	213 P-0	200 P-7
37 STOP	38 TYR	39 TYR	32 TRP
231 P-45	232 P-42	233 P-12	220 P-11
45 SER	46 SER	47 SER	40 LEU
311 P-18	312 P-21	313 P-51	300 P-52
53 GLN	54 HIS	55 HIS	48 ARG
331 P-30	332 P-25	333 P-63	320 P-56
61 PRO	62 PRO	63 PRO	56 LEU

Column 7, 1st Row

013 P-7	000 P-0	001 P-38	002 P-33
7 ASP	0 GLY	1 GLY	2 GLY
033 P-11	020 P-12	021 P-42	022 P-45
15 ALA	8 VAL	9 VAL	10 VAL
113 P-52	100 P-51	101 P-21	102 P-18
23 ASN	16 ARG	17 ARG	18 SER
133 P-56	120 P-63	121 P-25	122 P-30
31 THR	24 MET	25 ILE	26 ILE

Column 5, 6th Row

231 P-45 — 45 SER	232 P-42 — 46 SER	233 P-12 — 47 SER	220 P-11 — 40 LEU
311 P-18 — 53 GLN	312 P-21 — 54 HIS	313 P-51 — 55 HIS	300 P-52 — 48 ARG
331 P-30 — 61 PRO	332 P-25 — 62 PRO	333 P-63 — 63 PRO	320 P-56 — 56 LEU
011 P-38 — 5 GLU	012 P-33 — 6 ASP	013 P-7 — 7 ASP	000 P-0 — 0 GLY

Column 7, 8th Row

333 P-63 — 63 PRO	320 P-56 — 56 LEU	321 P-30 — 57 LEU	322 P-25 — 58 LEU
013 P-7 — 7 ASP	000 P-0 — 0 GLY	001 P-38 — 1 GLY	002 P-33 — 2 GLY
033 P-11 — 15 ALA	020 P-12 — 8 VAL	021 P-42 — 9 VAL	022 P-45 — 10 VAL
113 P-52 — 23 ASN	100 P-51 — 16 ARG	101 P-21 — 17 ARG	102 P-18 — 18 SER

Column 5, 7th Row

311 P-18	312 P-21	313 P-51	300 P-52
53 GLN	54 HIS	55 HIS	48 ARG
331 P-30	332 P-25	333 P-63	320 P-56
61 PRO	62 PRO	63 PRO	56 LEU
011 P-88	012 P-93	013 P-7	000 P-0
5 GLU	6 ASP	7 ASP	0 GLY
031 P-42	032 P-45	033 P-11	020 P-12
13 ALA	14 ALA	15 ALA	8 VAL

Column 7, 7th Row

313 P-51	300 P-52	301 P-18	302 P-21
55 HIS	48 ARG	49 ARG	50 ARG
333 P-63	320 P-56	321 P-30	322 P-25
63 PRO	56 LEU	57 LEU	58 LEU
013 P-7	000 P-0	001 P-88	002 P-93
7 ASP	0 GLY	1 GLY	2 GLY
033 P-11	020 P-12	021 P-42	022 P-45
15 ALA	8 VAL	9 VAL	10 VAL

Column 5, 8th Row

331 P-30	332 P-25	333 P-63	320 P-56
61 PRO	62 PRO	63 PRO	56 LEU
011 P-38	012 P-33	013 P-7	000 P-0
5 GLU	6 ASP	7 ASP	0 GLY
031 P-42	032 P-45	033 P-11	020 P-12
13 ALA	14 ALA	15 ALA	8 VAL
111 P-21	112 P-18	113 P-52	100 P-51
21 LYS	22 ASN	23 ASN	18 ARG

Column 7, 6th Row

233 P-12	220 P-11	221 P-45	222 P-42
47 SER	40 LEU	41 LEU	42 PHE
313 P-51	300 P-52	301 P-18	302 P-21
55 HIS	48 ARG	49 ARG	50 ARG
333 P-63	320 P-56	321 P-30	322 P-25
63 PRO	56 LEU	57 LEU	58 LEU
013 P-7	000 P-0	001 P-38	002 P-33
7 ASP	0 GLY	1 GLY	2 GLY

Column 6, 1st Row

012 P-93	013 P-7	000 P-0	001 P-68
6 ASP	7 ASP	0 GLY	1 GLY
032 P-45	033 P-11	020 P-12	021 P-42
14 ALA	15 ALA	8 VAL	9 VAL
112 P-18	113 P-52	100 P-51	101 P-21
22 ASN	23 ASN	16 ARG	17 ARG
132 P-30	133 P-56	120 P-63	121 P-25
30 THR	31 THR	24 MET	25 ILE

Column 6, 5th Row

212 P-98	213 P-0	200 P-7	201 P-93
38 TYR	39 TYR	32 TRP	33 STOP
232 P-42	233 P-12	220 P-11	221 P-45
46 SER	47 SER	40 LEU	41 LEU
312 P-21	313 P-51	300 P-52	301 P-18
54 HIS	55 HIS	48 ARG	49 ARG
332 P-25	333 P-63	320 P-56	321 P-30
62 PRO	63 PRO	56 LEU	57 LEU

Column 6, 2nd Row

032 P-45	093 P-11	020 P-12	021 P-42
14 ALA	15 ALA	8 VAL	9 VAL
112 P-18	113 P-52	100 P-51	101 P-21
22 ASN	23 ASN	16 ARG	17 ARG
132 P-90	133 P-56	120 P-63	121 P-25
30 THR	31 THR	24 MET	25 ILE
212 P-98	213 P-0	200 P-7	201 P-93
38 TYR	39 TYR	32 TRP	33 STOP

Column 6, 4th Row

132 P-90	133 P-56	120 P-63	121 P-25
30 THR	31 THR	24 MET	25 ILE
212 P-98	213 P-0	200 P-7	201 P-93
38 TYR	39 TYR	32 TRP	33 STOP
232 P-42	233 P-12	220 P-11	221 P-45
46 SER	47 SER	40 LEU	41 LEU
312 P-21	313 P-51	300 P-52	301 P-18
54 HIS	55 HIS	48 ARG	49 ARG

Column 6, 3rd Row

	112	P-18		115	P-52		100	P-51		101	P-21
	22	ASN		23	ASN		16	ARG		17	ARG
	132	P-30		133	P-56		120	P-63		121	P-25
	30	THR		31	THR		24	MET		25	ILE
	212	P-38		213	P-0		200	P-7		201	P-33
	38	TYR		39	TYR		32	TRP		33	STOP
	232	P-42		233	P-12		220	P-11		221	P-45
	46	SER		47	SER		40	LEU		41	LEU

Column 6, 3rd Row

	112	P-18		115	P-52		100	P-51		101	P-21
	22	ASN		23	ASN		16	ARG		17	ARG
	132	P-30		133	P-56		120	P-63		121	P-25
	30	THR		31	THR		24	MET		25	ILE
	212	P-38		213	P-0		200	P-7		201	P-33
	38	TYR		39	TYR		32	TRP		33	STOP
	232	P-42		233	P-12		220	P-11		221	P-45
	46	SER		47	SER		40	LEU		41	LEU

Column 6, 6th Row

232 P-42	233 P-12	220 P-11	221 P-45
46 SER	47 SER	40 LEU	41 LEU
312 P-21	313 P-51	300 P-52	301 P-18
54 HIS	55 HIS	48 ARG	49 ARG
332 P-25	333 P-63	320 P-56	321 P-30
62 PRO	63 PRO	56 LEU	57 LEU
012 P-33	013 P-7	000 P-0	001 P-38
6 ASP	7 ASP	0 GLY	1 GLY

Column 6, 8th Row

332 P-25	333 P-63	320 P-56	321 P-30
62 PRO	63 PRO	56 LEU	57 LEU
012 P-33	013 P-7	000 P-0	001 P-38
6 ASP	7 ASP	0 GLY	1 GLY
032 P-45	033 P-11	020 P-12	021 P-42
14 ALA	15 ALA	8 VAL	9 VAL
112 P-18	113 P-52	100 P-51	101 P-21
22 ASN	23 ASN	16 ARG	17 ARG

Column 6, 7th Row

312 P-21		313 P-51		300 P-52		301 P-18	
54 HIS		55 HIS		48 ARG		49 ARG	
332 P-25		333 P-63		320 P-56		321 P-30	
62 PRO		63 PRO		56 LEU		57 LEU	
012 P-33		013 P-7		000 P-0		001 P-38	
6 ASP		7 ASP		0 GLY		1 GLY	
032 P-45		033 P-11		020 P-12		021 P-42	
14 ALA		15 ALA		8 VAL		9 VAL	

Column 6, 7th Row

312 P-21		313 P-51		300 P-52		301 P-18	
54 HIS		55 HIS		48 ARG		49 ARG	
332 P-25		333 P-63		320 P-56		321 P-30	
62 PRO		63 PRO		56 LEU		57 LEU	
012 P-33		013 P-7		000 P-0		001 P-38	
6 ASP		7 ASP		0 GLY		1 GLY	
032 P-45		033 P-11		020 P-12		021 P-42	
14 ALA		15 ALA		8 VAL		9 VAL	

8: Binary Pairs in Position

Column 0, 1st Row

000 P-0 / 0 GLY					003 P-7 / 3 GLY
		023 P-11 / 11 VAL	020 P-12 / 8 VAL		
		102 P-18 / 18 SER		101 P-21 / 17 ARG	
	121 P-25 / 25 ILE			122 P-30 / 26 ILE	
	002 P-33 / 2 GLY			001 P-38 / 1 GLY	
		021 P-42 / 9 VAL		022 P-45 / 10 VAL	
		100 P-51 / 16 ARG	103 P-52 / 19 SER		
123 P-56 / 27 ILE					120 P-63 / 24 MET

Column 4, 5th Row

333 P-63 / 63 PRO					330 P-56 / 60 PRO
		310 P-52 / 52 GLN	313 P-51 / 55 HIS		
		231 P-45 / 45 SER		232 P-42 / 46 SER	
	212 P-38 / 38 TYR			211 P-33 / 37 STOP	
	331 P-30 / 61 PRO			332 P-25 / 62 PRO	
		312 P-21 / 54 HIS		311 P-18 / 53 GLN	
		233 P-12 / 47 SER	230 P-11 / 44 SER		
210 P-7 / 36 STOP					213 P-0 / 39 TYR

Column 0, 2nd Row

203 P-0 / 35 CYS							200 P-7 / 32 TRP
			023 P-11 / 11 VAL	020 P-12 / 8 VAL			
		102 P-18 / 18 SER			101 P-21 / 17 ARG		
	121 P-25 / 25 ILE					122 P-30 / 26 ILE	
	201 P-33 / 33 STOP					202 P-38 / 34 CYS	
		021 P-42 / 9 VAL			022 P-45 / 10 VAL		
			100 P-51 / 16 ARG	103 P-52 / 19 SER			
123 P-56 / 27 ILE							120 P-63 / 24 MET

Column 4, 4th Row

130 P-63 / 28 THR							133 P-56 / 31 THR
			310 P-52 / 52 GLN	313 P-51 / 55 HIS			
		231 P-45 / 45 SER			232 P-42 / 46 SER		
	212 P-38 / 38 TYR					211 P-33 / 37 STOP	
	132 P-30 / 30 THR					131 P-25 / 29 THR	
		312 P-21 / 54 HIS			311 P-18 / 53 GLN		
			233 P-12 / 47 SER	230 P-11 / 44 SER			
210 P-7 / 36 STOP							213 P-0 / 39 TYR

Column 0, 3rd Row

203 P-0 / 35 CYS						200 P-7 / 32 TRP
			220 P-11 / 40 LEU	223 P-12 / 43 PHE		
		102 P-18 / 18 SER			101 P-21 / 17 ARG	
	121 P-25 / 25 ILE				122 P-30 / 26 ILE	
	201 P-33 / 33 STOP				202 P-38 / 34 CYS	
		222 P-42 / 42 PHE			221 P-45 / 41 LEU	
			100 P-51 / 16 ARG	103 P-52 / 19 SER		
123 P-56 / 27 ILE						120 P-63 / 24 MET

Column 4, 3rd Row

130 P-63 / 28 THR						133 P-56 / 31 THR
			113 P-52 / 23 ASN	110 P-51 / 20 LYS		
		231 P-45 / 45 SER			232 P-42 / 46 SER	
	212 P-38 / 38 TYR				211 P-33 / 37 STOP	
	132 P-30 / 30 THR				131 P-25 / 29 THR	
		111 P-21 / 21 LYS			112 P-18 / 22 ASN	
			233 P-12 / 47 SER	230 P-11 / 44 SER		
210 P-7 / 36 STOP						213 P-0 / 39 TYR

Column 0, 4th Row

203 P-0 35 CYS							200 P-7 32 TRP
			220 P-11 40 LEU	223 P-12 43 PHE			
		301 P-18 49 ARG			302 P-21 50 ARG		
	121 P-25 25 ILE					122 P-30 26 ILE	
	201 P-33 33 STOP					202 P-38 34 CYS	
		222 P-42 42 PHE			221 P-45 41 LEU		
			303 P-51 51 ARG	300 P-52 48 ARG			
123 P-56 27 ILE							120 P-63 24 MET

Column 4, 2nd Row

130 P-63 28 THR							133 P-56 31 THR
			113 P-52 23 ASN	110 P-51 20 LYS			
		032 P-45 14 ALA			031 P-42 13 ALA		
	212 P-38 38 TYR					211 P-33 37 STOP	
	132 P-30 30 THR					131 P-25 29 THR	
		111 P-21 21 LYS			112 P-18 22 ASN		
			030 P-12 12 ALA	033 P-11 15 ALA			
210 P-7 36 STOP							213 P-0 39 TYR

Column 0, 5th Row

203 P-0 — 35 CYS						200 P-7 — 32 TRP
			220 P-11 — 40 LEU	223 P-12 — 43 PHE		
		301 P-18 — 49 ARG			302 P-21 — 50 ARG	
	322 P-25 — 58 LEU				321 P-30 — 57 LEU	
	201 P-33 — 33 STOP				202 P-38 — 34 CYS	
		222 P-42 — 42 PHE			221 P-45 — 41 LEU	
			303 P-51 — 51 ARG	300 P-52 — 48 ARG		
320 P-56 — 56 LEU						323 P-63 — 59 LEU

Column 4, 1st Row

130 P-63 — 28 THR						133 P-56 — 31 THR
			113 P-52 — 23 ASN	110 P-51 — 20 LYS		
		032 P-45 — 14 ALA			031 P-42 — 13 ALA	
	011 P-38 — 5 GLU				012 P-33 — 6 ASP	
	132 P-30 — 30 THR				131 P-25 — 29 THR	
		111 P-21 — 21 LYS			112 P-18 — 22 ASN	
			030 P-12 — 12 ALA	033 P-11 — 15 ALA		
013 P-7 — 7 ASP						010 P-0 — 4 GLU

Column 0, 6th Row

000 P-0 — 0 GLY					003 P-7 — 3 GLY
		220 P-11 — 40 LEU	223 P-12 — 43 PHE		
	301 P-18 — 49 ARG			302 P-21 — 50 ARG	
	322 P-25 — 58 LEU			321 P-30 — 57 LEU	
	002 P-33 — 2 GLY			001 P-38 — 1 GLY	
	222 P-42 — 42 PHE		221 P-45 — 41 LEU		
		303 P-51 — 51 ARG	300 P-52 — 48 ARG		
320 P-56 — 56 LEU					323 P-63 — 59 LEU

Column 4, 8th Row

333 P-63 — 63 PRO					330 P-56 — 60 PRO
		113 P-52 — 23 ASN	110 P-51 — 20 LYS		
	032 P-45 — 14 ALA			031 P-42 — 13 ALA	
	011 P-38 — 5 GLU			012 P-33 — 6 ASP	
	331 P-30 — 61 PRO			332 P-25 — 62 PRO	
	111 P-21 — 21 LYS		112 P-18 — 22 ASN		
		030 P-12 — 12 ALA	033 P-11 — 15 ALA		
013 P-7 — 7 ASP					010 P-0 — 4 GLU

Column 0, 7th Row

000 P-0 0 GLY					003 P-7 3 GLY
		023 P-11 11 VAL	020 P-12 8 VAL		
	301 P-18 49 ARG			302 P-21 50 ARG	
	322 P-25 58 LEU			321 P-30 57 LEU	
	002 P-33 2 GLY			001 P-38 1 GLY	
	021 P-42 9 VAL		022 P-45 10 VAL		
		303 P-51 51 ARG	300 P-52 48 ARG		
320 P-56 56 LEU					323 P-63 59 LEU

Column 4, 7th Row

333 P-63 63 PRO					330 P-56 60 PRO
		310 P-52 52 GLN	313 P-51 55 HIS		
	032 P-45 14 ALA			031 P-42 13 ALA	
	011 P-38 5 GLU			012 P-33 6 ASP	
	331 P-30 61 PRO			332 P-25 62 PRO	
	312 P-21 54 HIS			311 P-18 53 GLN	
		030 P-12 12 ALA	033 P-11 15 ALA		
013 P-7 7 ASP					010 P-0 4 GLU

Column 0, 8th Row

000 P-0 0 GLY						003 P-7 3 GLY
			023 P-11 11 VAL	020 P-12 8 VAL		
		102 P-18 18 SER			101 P-21 17 ARG	
	322 P-25 58 LEU				321 P-30 57 LEU	
	002 P-33 2 GLY				001 P-38 1 GLY	
		021 P-42 9 VAL			022 P-45 10 VAL	
			100 P-51 16 ARG	103 P-52 19 SER		
320 P-56 56 LEU						323 P-63 59 LEU

Column 4, 6th Row

333 P-63 63 PRO						330 P-56 60 PRO
			310 P-52 52 GLN	313 P-51 55 HIS		
		231 P-45 45 SER			232 P-42 46 SER	
	011 P-38 5 GLU				012 P-33 6 ASP	
	331 P-30 61 PRO				332 P-25 62 PRO	
		312 P-21 54 HIS			311 P-18 53 GLN	
			233 P-12 47 SER	230 P-11 44 SER		
013 P-7 7 ASP						010 P-0 4 GLU

Column 1, 1st Row

010 P-0 4 GLU					003 P-7 3 GLY
		023 P-11 11 VAL	030 P-12 12 ALA		
		102 P-18 18 SER		101 P-21 17 ARG	
	121 P-25 25 ILE				122 P-30 26 ILE
	002 P-33 2 GLY				001 P-38 1 GLY
		021 P-42 9 VAL		022 P-45 10 VAL	
		110 P-51 20 LYS	103 P-52 19 SER		
123 P-56 27 ILE					130 P-63 28 THR

Column 3, 5th Row

323 P-63 59 LEU					330 P-56 60 PRO
		310 P-52 52 GLN	303 P-51 51 ARG		
		231 P-45 45 SER		232 P-42 46 SER	
	212 P-38 38 TYR				211 P-33 37 STOP
	331 P-30 61 PRO				332 P-25 62 PRO
		312 P-21 54 HIS		311 P-18 53 GLN	
		223 P-12 43 PHE	230 P-11 44 SER		
210 P-7 36 STOP					203 P-0 35 CYS

Column 1, 2nd Row

203 P-0 35 CYS							210 P-7 36 STOP
			023 P-11 11 VAL	030 P-12 12 ALA			
		102 P-18 18 SER			101 P-21 17 ARG		
	121 P-25 25 ILE					122 P-30 26 ILE	
	201 P-33 33 STOP					202 P-38 34 CYS	
		021 P-42 9 VAL			022 P-45 10 VAL		
			110 P-51 20 LYS	103 P-52 19 SER			
123 P-56 27 ILE							130 P-63 28 THR

Column 3, 4th Row

130 P-63 28 THR							123 P-56 27 ILE
			310 P-52 52 GLN	303 P-51 51 ARG			
		231 P-45 45 SER			232 P-42 46 SER		
	212 P-38 38 TYR					211 P-33 37 STOP	
	132 P-30 30 THR					131 P-25 29 THR	
		312 P-21 54 HIS			311 P-18 53 GLN		
			223 P-12 43 PHE	230 P-11 44 SER			
210 P-7 36 STOP							203 P-0 35 CYS

Column 1, 3rd Row

203 P-0 35 CYS						210 P-7 36 STOP
		230 P-11 44 SER	223 P-12 43 PHE			
	102 P-18 18 SER			101 P-21 17 ARG		
	121 P-25 25 ILE				122 P-30 26 ILE	
	201 P-33 33 STOP				202 P-38 34 CYS	
	222 P-42 42 PHE			221 P-45 41 LEU		
		110 P-51 20 LYS	103 P-52 19 SER			
123 P-56 27 ILE						130 P-63 28 THR

Column 3, 3rd Row

130 P-63 28 THR						123 P-56 27 ILE
		103 P-52 19 SER	110 P-51 20 LYS			
	231 P-45 45 SER			232 P-42 46 SER		
	212 P-38 38 TYR				211 P-33 37 STOP	
	132 P-30 30 THR				131 P-25 29 THR	
	111 P-21 21 LYS			112 P-18 22 ASN		
		223 P-12 43 PHE	230 P-11 44 SER			
210 P-7 36 STOP						203 P-0 35 CYS

Column 1, 4th Row

203 P-0 35 CYS						210 P-7 36 STOP
		230 P-11 44 SER	223 P-12 43 PHE			
		301 P-18 49 ARG		302 P-21 50 ARG		
	121 P-25 25 ILE				122 P-30 26 ILE	
	201 P-33 33 STOP				202 P-38 34 CYS	
		222 P-42 42 PHE		221 P-45 41 LEU		
		303 P-51 51 ARG	310 P-52 52 GLN			
123 P-56 27 ILE						130 P-63 28 THR

Column 3, 2nd Row

130 P-63 28 THR						123 P-56 27 ILE
		103 P-52 19 SER	110 P-51 20 LYS			
	032 P-45 14 ALA			031 P-42 13 ALA		
	212 P-38 38 TYR				211 P-33 37 STOP	
	132 P-30 30 THR				131 P-25 29 THR	
		111 P-21 21 LYS		112 P-18 22 ASN		
		030 P-12 12 ALA	023 P-11 11 VAL			
210 P-7 36 STOP						203 P-0 35 CYS

Column 1, 5th Row

203 P-0 / 35 CYS						210 P-7 / 36 STOP
			230 P-11 / 44 SER	223 P-12 / 43 PHE		
		301 P-18 / 49 ARG			302 P-21 / 50 ARG	
	322 P-25 / 58 LEU				321 P-30 / 57 LEU	
	201 P-33 / 33 STOP				202 P-38 / 34 CYS	
		222 P-42 / 42 PHE			221 P-45 / 41 LEU	
			303 P-51 / 51 ARG	310 P-52 / 52 GLN		
330 P-56 / 60 PRO						323 P-63 / 59 LEU

Column 3, 1st Row

130 P-63 / 28 THR						123 P-56 / 27 ILE
			103 P-52 / 19 SER	110 P-51 / 20 LYS		
		032 P-45 / 14 ALA			031 P-42 / 13 ALA	
	011 P-38 / 5 GLU				012 P-33 / 6 ASP	
	132 P-30 / 30 THR				131 P-25 / 29 THR	
		111 P-21 / 21 LYS			112 P-18 / 22 ASN	
			030 P-12 / 12 ALA	023 P-11 / 11 VAL		
003 P-7 / 3 GLY						010 P-0 / 4 GLU

Column 1, 6th Row

010 P-0 4 GLU						003 P-7 3 GLY
			230 P-11 44 SER	223 P-12 43 PHE		
		301 P-18 49 ARG			302 P-21 50 ARG	
	322 P-25 58 LEU					321 P-30 57 LEU
	002 P-33 2 GLY					001 P-38 1 GLY
		222 P-42 42 PHE			221 P-45 41 LEU	
			303 P-51 51 ARG	310 P-52 52 GLN		
330 P-56 60 PRO						323 P-63 59 LEU

Column 3, 8th Row

323 P-63 59 LEU						330 P-56 60 PRO
			103 P-52 19 SER	110 P-51 20 LYS		
		032 P-45 14 ALA			031 P-42 13 ALA	
	011 P-38 5 GLU					012 P-33 6 ASP
	331 P-30 61 PRO					332 P-25 62 PRO
		111 P-21 21 LYS			112 P-18 22 ASN	
			030 P-12 12 ALA	023 P-11 11 VAL		
003 P-7 3 GLY						010 P-0 4 GLU

Column 1, 7th Row

010 P-0 — 4 GLU							003 P-7 — 3 GLY
			023 P-11 — 11 VAL	030 P-12 — 12 ALA			
		301 P-18 — 49 ARG			302 P-21 — 50 ARG		
	322 P-25 — 58 LEU					321 P-30 — 57 LEU	
	002 P-33 — 2 GLY					001 P-38 — 1 GLY	
		021 P-42 — 9 VAL			022 P-45 — 10 VAL		
			303 P-51 — 51 ARG	310 P-52 — 52 GLN			
330 P-56 — 60 PRO							323 P-63 — 59 LEU

Column 3, 7th Row

323 P-63 — 59 LEU							330 P-56 — 60 PRO
			310 P-52 — 52 GLN	303 P-51 — 51 ARG			
		032 P-45 — 14 ALA			031 P-42 — 13 ALA		
	011 P-38 — 5 GLU					012 P-33 — 6 ASP	
	331 P-30 — 61 PRO					332 P-25 — 62 PRO	
		312 P-21 — 54 HIS			311 P-18 — 53 GLN		
			030 P-12 — 12 ALA	023 P-11 — 11 VAL			
003 P-7 — 3 GLY							010 P-0 — 4 GLU

Column 1, 8th Row

010 P-0 4 GLU						003 P-7 3 GLY
		023 P-11 11 VAL	030 P-12 12 ALA			
	102 P-18 18 SER			101 P-21 17 ARG		
	322 P-25 58 LEU				321 P-30 57 LEU	
	002 P-33 2 GLY				001 P-38 1 GLY	
	021 P-42 9 VAL			022 P-45 10 VAL		
		110 P-51 20 LYS	103 P-52 19 SER			
330 P-56 60 PRO						323 P-63 59 LEU

Column 3, 6th Row

323 P-63 59 LEU						330 P-56 60 PRO
		310 P-52 52 GLN	303 P-51 51 ARG			
	231 P-45 45 SER			232 P-42 46 SER		
	011 P-38 5 GLU				012 P-33 6 ASP	
	331 P-30 61 PRO				332 P-25 62 PRO	
	312 P-21 54 HIS			311 P-18 53 GLN		
		223 P-12 43 PHE	230 P-11 44 SER			
003 P-7 3 GLY						010 P-0 4 GLU

Column 2, 1st Row

010 P-0 4 GLU						003 P-7 3 GLY
			023 P-11 11 VAL	030 P-12 12 ALA		
		102 P-18 18 SER			111 P-21 21 LYS	
	131 P-25 29 THR					122 P-30 26 ILE
	002 P-33 2 GLY					011 P-38 5 GLU
		031 P-42 13 ALA			022 P-45 10 VAL	
			110 P-51 20 LYS	103 P-52 19 SER		
123 P-56 27 ILE						130 P-63 28 THR

Column 2, 5th Row

323 P-63 59 LEU						330 P-56 60 PRO
			310 P-52 52 GLN	303 P-51 51 ARG		
		231 P-45 45 SER			222 P-42 42 PHE	
	202 P-38 34 CYS					211 P-33 37 STOP
	331 P-30 61 PRO					322 P-25 58 LEU
		302 P-21 50 ARG			311 P-18 53 GLN	
			223 P-12 43 PHE	230 P-11 44 SER		
210 P-7 36 STOP						203 P-0 35 CYS

Column 2, 2nd Row

203 P-0 — 35 CYS					210 P-7 — 36 STOP
		023 P-11 — 11 VAL	030 P-12 — 12 ALA		
		102 P-18 — 18 SER		111 P-21 — 21 LYS	
	131 P-25 — 29 THR			122 P-30 — 26 ILE	
	211 P-33 — 37 STOP			202 P-38 — 34 CYS	
		031 P-42 — 13 ALA		022 P-45 — 10 VAL	
		110 P-51 — 20 LYS	103 P-52 — 19 SER		
123 P-56 — 27 ILE					130 P-63 — 28 THR

Column 2, 4th Row

130 P-63 — 28 THR					123 P-56 — 27 ILE
		310 P-52 — 52 GLN	303 P-51 — 51 ARG		
		231 P-45 — 45 SER		222 P-42 — 42 PHE	
	202 P-38 — 34 CYS			211 P-33 — 37 STOP	
	122 P-30 — 26 ILE			131 P-25 — 29 THR	
		302 P-21 — 50 ARG		311 P-18 — 53 GLN	
		223 P-12 — 43 PHE	230 P-11 — 44 SER		
210 P-7 — 36 STOP					203 P-0 — 35 CYS

Column 2, 3rd Row

203 P-0 / 35 CYS							210 P-7 / 36 STOP
			230 P-11 / 44 SER	223 P-12 / 43 PHE			
		102 P-18 / 18 SER			111 P-21 / 21 LYS		
	131 P-25 / 29 THR					122 P-30 / 26 ILE	
	211 P-33 / 37 STOP					202 P-38 / 34 CYS	
		222 P-42 / 42 PHE			231 P-45 / 45 SER		
			110 P-51 / 20 LYS	103 P-52 / 19 SER			
123 P-56 / 27 ILE							130 P-63 / 28 THR

Column 2, 3rd Row (reversed)

130 P-63 / 28 THR							123 P-56 / 27 ILE
			103 P-52 / 19 SER	110 P-51 / 20 LYS			
		231 P-45 / 45 SER			222 P-42 / 42 PHE		
	202 P-38 / 34 CYS					211 P-33 / 37 STOP	
	122 P-30 / 26 ILE					131 P-25 / 29 THR	
		111 P-21 / 21 LYS			102 P-18 / 18 SER		
			223 P-12 / 43 PHE	230 P-11 / 44 SER			
210 P-7 / 36 STOP							203 P-0 / 35 CYS

Column 2, 6th Row

010 P-0 4 GLU						003 P-7 3 GLY
			230 P-11 44 SER	223 P-12 43 PHE		
		311 P-18 53 GLN			302 P-21 50 ARG	
	322 P-25 58 LEU					331 P-30 61 PRO
	002 P-33 2 GLY					011 P-38 5 GLU
		222 P-42 42 PHE			231 P-45 45 SER	
			303 P-51 51 ARG	310 P-52 52 GLN		
330 P-56 60 PRO						323 P-63 59 LEU

Column 2, 8th Row

323 P-63 59 LEU						330 P-56 60 PRO
			103 P-52 19 SER	110 P-51 20 LYS		
		022 P-45 10 VAL			031 P-42 13 ALA	
	011 P-38 5 GLU				002 P-33 2 GLY	
	331 P-30 61 PRO				322 P-25 58 LEU	
		111 P-21 21 LYS			102 P-18 18 SER	
			030 P-12 12 ALA	023 P-11 11 VAL		
003 P-7 3 GLY						010 P-0 4 GLU

Column 2, 7th Row

010 P-0 / 4 GLU							003 P-7 / 3 GLY
			023 P-11 / 11 VAL	030 P-12 / 12 ALA			
		311 P-18 / 53 GLN			302 P-21 / 50 ARG		
	322 P-25 / 58 LEU					331 P-30 / 61 PRO	
	002 P-33 / 2 GLY					011 P-38 / 5 GLU	
		031 P-42 / 13 ALA			022 P-45 / 10 VAL		
			303 P-51 / 51 ARG	310 P-52 / 52 GLN			
330 P-56 / 60 PRO							323 P-63 / 59 LEU

Column 2, 7th Row (reversed)

323 P-63 / 59 LEU							330 P-56 / 60 PRO
			310 P-52 / 52 GLN	303 P-51 / 51 ARG			
		022 P-45 / 10 VAL			031 P-42 / 13 ALA		
	011 P-38 / 5 GLU					002 P-33 / 2 GLY	
	331 P-30 / 61 PRO					322 P-25 / 58 LEU	
		302 P-21 / 50 ARG			311 P-18 / 53 GLN		
			030 P-12 / 12 ALA	023 P-11 / 11 VAL			
003 P-7 / 3 GLY							010 P-0 / 4 GLU

Column 5, 1st Row

000 P-0 0 GLY							013 P-7 7 ASP
			033 P-11 15 ALA	020 P-12 8 VAL			
		112 P-18 22 ASN			111 P-21 21 LYS		
	131 P-25 29 THR					132 P-30 30 THR	
	012 P-33 6 ASP					011 P-38 5 GLU	
		031 P-42 13 ALA			032 P-45 14 ALA		
			100 P-51 16 ARG	113 P-52 23 ASN			
133 P-56 31 THR							120 P-63 24 MET

Column 7, 5th Row

333 P-63 63 PRO							320 P-56 56 LEU
			300 P-52 48 ARG	313 P-51 55 HIS			
		221 P-45 41 LEU			222 P-42 42 PHE		
	202 P-38 34 CYS					201 P-33 33 STOP	
	321 P-30 57 LEU					322 P-25 58 LEU	
		302 P-21 50 ARG			301 P-18 49 ARG		
			233 P-12 47 SER	220 P-11 40 LEU			
200 P-7 32 TRP							213 P-0 39 TYR

Column 5, 2nd Row

213 P-0 — 39 TYR						200 P-7 — 32 TRP
			033 P-11 — 15 ALA	020 P-12 — 8 VAL		
		112 P-18 — 22 ASN			111 P-21 — 21 LYS	
	131 P-25 — 29 THR				132 P-30 — 30 THR	
	211 P-33 — 37 STOP				212 P-38 — 38 TYR	
		031 P-42 — 13 ALA			032 P-45 — 14 ALA	
			100 P-51 — 16 ARG	113 P-52 — 23 ASN		
133 P-56 — 31 THR						120 P-63 — 24 MET

Column 7, 4th Row

120 P-63 — 24 MET						133 P-56 — 31 THR
			300 P-52 — 48 ARG	313 P-51 — 55 HIS		
		221 P-45 — 41 LEU			222 P-42 — 42 PHE	
	202 P-38 — 34 CYS				201 P-33 — 33 STOP	
	122 P-30 — 26 ILE				121 P-25 — 25 ILE	
		302 P-21 — 50 ARG			301 P-18 — 49 ARG	
			233 P-12 — 47 SER	220 P-11 — 40 LEU		
200 P-7 — 32 TRP						213 P-0 — 39 TYR

Column 5, 3rd Row

213 P-0 39 TYR						200 P-7 32 TRP
			220 P-11 40 LEU	233 P-12 47 SER		
		112 P-18 22 ASN			111 P-21 21 LYS	
	131 P-25 29 THR				132 P-30 30 THR	
	211 P-33 37 STOP				212 P-38 38 TYR	
		232 P-42 46 SER			231 P-45 45 SER	
			100 P-51 16 ARG	113 P-52 23 ASN		
133 P-56 31 THR						120 P-63 24 MET

Column 7, 3rd Row

120 P-63 24 MET						133 P-56 31 THR
			113 P-52 23 ASN	100 P-51 16 ARG		
		221 P-45 41 LEU			222 P-42 42 PHE	
	202 P-38 34 CYS				201 P-33 33 STOP	
	122 P-30 26 ILE				121 P-25 25 ILE	
		101 P-21 17 ARG			102 P-18 18 SER	
			233 P-12 47 SER	220 P-11 40 LEU		
200 P-7 32 TRP						213 P-0 39 TYR

Column 5, 4th Row

213 P-0 — 39 TYR					200 P-7 — 32 TRP
		220 P-11 — 40 LEU	233 P-12 — 47 SER		
		311 P-18 — 53 GLN		312 P-21 — 54 HIS	
	131 P-25 — 29 THR				132 P-30 — 30 THR
	211 P-33 — 37 STOP				212 P-38 — 38 TYR
		232 P-42 — 46 SER		231 P-45 — 45 SER	
		313 P-51 — 55 HIS	300 P-52 — 48 ARG		
133 P-56 — 31 THR					120 P-63 — 24 MET

Column 7, 2nd Row

120 P-63 — 24 MET					133 P-56 — 31 THR
		113 P-52 — 23 ASN	100 P-51 — 16 ARG		
		022 P-45 — 10 VAL		021 P-42 — 9 VAL	
	202 P-38 — 34 CYS				201 P-33 — 33 STOP
	122 P-30 — 26 ILE				121 P-25 — 25 ILE
		101 P-21 — 17 ARG		102 P-18 — 18 SER	
		020 P-12 — 8 VAL	033 P-11 — 15 ALA		
200 P-7 — 32 TRP					213 P-0 — 39 TYR

Column 5, 5th Row

213 P-0 39 TYR							200 P-7 32 TRP
			220 P-11 40 LEU	233 P-12 47 SER			
		311 P-18 53 GLN			312 P-21 54 HIS		
	332 P-25 62 PRO					331 P-30 61 PRO	
	211 P-33 37 STOP					212 P-38 38 TYR	
		232 P-42 46 SER			231 P-45 45 SER		
			313 P-51 55 HIS	300 P-52 48 ARG			
320 P-56 56 LEU							333 P-63 63 PRO

Column 7, 1st Row

120 P-63 24 MET							133 P-56 31 THR
			113 P-52 23 ASN	100 P-51 16 ARG			
		022 P-45 10 VAL			021 P-42 9 VAL		
	001 P-38 1 GLY					002 P-33 2 GLY	
	122 P-30 26 ILE					121 P-25 25 ILE	
		101 P-21 17 ARG			102 P-18 18 SER		
			020 P-12 8 VAL	033 P-11 15 ALA			
013 P-7 7 ASP							000 P-0 0 GLY

Column 5, 6th Row

000 P-0 / 0 GLY						013 P-7 / 7 ASP
			220 P-11 / 40 LEU	233 P-12 / 47 SER		
		311 P-18 / 53 GLN			312 P-21 / 54 HIS	
	332 P-25 / 62 PRO					331 P-30 / 61 PRO
	012 P-33 / 6 ASP					011 P-38 / 5 GLU
		232 P-42 / 46 SER			231 P-45 / 45 SER	
			313 P-51 / 55 HIS	300 P-52 / 48 ARG		
320 P-56 / 56 LEU						333 P-63 / 63 PRO

Column 7, 8th Row

333 P-63 / 63 PRO						320 P-56 / 56 LEU
			113 P-52 / 23 ASN	100 P-51 / 16 ARG		
		022 P-45 / 10 VAL			021 P-42 / 9 VAL	
	001 P-38 / 1 GLY					002 P-33 / 2 GLY
	321 P-30 / 57 LEU					322 P-25 / 58 LEU
		101 P-21 / 17 ARG			102 P-18 / 18 SER	
			020 P-12 / 8 VAL	033 P-11 / 15 ALA		
013 P-7 / 7 ASP						000 P-0 / 0 GLY

Column 5, 7th Row

-- 000 P-0 -- -- -- -- 0 GLY						-- 013 P-7 -- -- -- -- 7 ASP
			-- 033 P-11 -- -- -- -- 15 ALA	-- 020 P-12 -- -- -- -- 8 VAL		
		-- 311 P-18 -- -- -- -- 53 GLN			-- 312 P-21 -- -- -- -- 54 HIS	
	-- 332 P-25 -- -- -- -- 62 PRO				-- 331 P-30 -- -- -- -- 61 PRO	
	-- 012 P-33 -- -- -- -- 6 ASP				-- 011 P-38 -- -- -- -- 5 GLU	
		-- 031 P-42 -- -- -- -- 13 ALA			-- 032 P-45 -- -- -- -- 14 ALA	
			-- 313 P-51 -- -- -- -- 55 HIS	-- 300 P-52 -- -- -- -- 48 ARG		
-- 320 P-56 -- -- -- -- 56 LEU						-- 333 P-63 -- -- -- -- 63 PRO

Column 7, 7th Row

-- 333 P-63 -- -- -- -- 63 PRO						-- 320 P-56 -- -- -- -- 56 LEU
			-- 300 P-52 -- -- -- -- 48 ARG	-- 313 P-51 -- -- -- -- 55 HIS		
		-- 022 P-45 -- -- -- -- 10 VAL			-- 021 P-42 -- -- -- -- 9 VAL	
	-- 001 P-38 -- -- -- -- 1 GLY				-- 002 P-33 -- -- -- -- 2 GLY	
	-- 321 P-30 -- -- -- -- 57 LEU				-- 322 P-25 -- -- -- -- 58 LEU	
		-- 302 P-21 -- -- -- -- 50 ARG			-- 301 P-18 -- -- -- -- 49 ARG	
			-- 020 P-12 -- -- -- -- 8 VAL	-- 033 P-11 -- -- -- -- 15 ALA		
-- 013 P-7 -- -- -- -- 7 ASP						-- 000 P-0 -- -- -- -- 0 GLY

Column 5, 8th Row

000 P-0 0 GLY					013 P-7 7 ASP
		033 P-11 15 ALA	020 P-12 8 VAL		
	112 P-18 22 ASN			111 P-21 21 LYS	
	332 P-25 62 PRO				331 P-30 61 PRO
	012 P-33 6 ASP				011 P-38 5 GLU
		031 P-42 13 ALA		032 P-45 14 ALA	
		100 P-51 16 ARG	113 P-52 23 ASN		
320 P-56 56 LEU					333 P-63 63 PRO

Column 7, 6th Row

333 P-63 63 PRO					320 P-56 56 LEU
		300 P-52 48 ARG	313 P-51 55 HIS		
	221 P-45 41 LEU			222 P-42 42 PHE	
	001 P-38 1 GLY				002 P-33 2 GLY
	321 P-30 57 LEU				322 P-25 58 LEU
		302 P-21 50 ARG		301 P-18 49 ARG	
		233 P-12 47 SER	220 P-11 40 LEU		
013 P-7 7 ASP					000 P-0 0 GLY

Column 6, 1st Row

000 P-0 0 GLY						013 P-7 7 ASP
			033 P-11 15 ALA	020 P-12 8 VAL		
		112 P-18 22 ASN			101 P-21 17 ARG	
	121 P-25 25 ILE					132 P-30 30 THR
	012 P-33 6 ASP					001 P-38 1 GLY
		021 P-42 9 VAL			032 P-45 14 ALA	
			100 P-51 16 ARG	113 P-52 23 ASN		
133 P-56 31 THR						120 P-63 24 MET

Column 6, 5th Row

333 P-63 63 PRO						320 P-56 56 LEU
			300 P-52 48 ARG	313 P-51 55 HIS		
		221 P-45 41 LEU			232 P-42 46 SER	
	212 P-38 38 TYR					201 P-33 33 STOP
	321 P-30 57 LEU					332 P-25 62 PRO
		312 P-21 54 HIS			301 P-18 49 ARG	
			233 P-12 47 SER	220 P-11 40 LEU		
200 P-7 32 TRP						213 P-0 39 TYR

Column 6, 2nd Row

213 P-0 39 TYR						200 P-7 32 TRP
			033 P-11 15 ALA	020 P-12 8 VAL		
		112 P-18 22 ASN			101 P-21 17 ARG	
	121 P-25 25 ILE				132 P-30 30 THR	
	201 P-33 33 STOP				212 P-38 38 TYR	
		021 P-42 9 VAL			032 P-45 14 ALA	
			100 P-51 16 ARG	113 P-52 23 ASN		
133 P-56 31 THR						120 P-63 24 MET

Column 6, 4th Row

120 P-63 24 MET						133 P-56 31 THR
			300 P-52 48 ARG	313 P-51 55 HIS		
		221 P-45 41 LEU			232 P-42 46 SER	
	212 P-38 38 TYR				201 P-33 33 STOP	
	132 P-30 30 THR				121 P-25 25 ILE	
		312 P-21 54 HIS			301 P-18 49 ARG	
			233 P-12 47 SER	220 P-11 40 LEU		
200 P-7 32 TRP						213 P-0 39 TYR

Column 6, 3rd Row

213 P-0 — 39 TYR							200 P-7 — 32 TRP
			220 P-11 — 40 LEU	233 P-12 — 47 SER			
		112 P-18 — 22 ASN			101 P-21 — 17 ARG		
	121 P-25 — 25 ILE					132 P-30 — 30 THR	
	201 P-33 — 33 STOP					212 P-38 — 38 TYR	
		232 P-42 — 46 SER			221 P-45 — 41 LEU		
			100 P-51 — 16 ARG	113 P-52 — 23 ASN			
133 P-56 — 31 THR							120 P-63 — 24 MET

Column 6, 3rd Row (reversed)

120 P-63 — 24 MET							133 P-56 — 31 THR
			113 P-52 — 23 ASN	100 P-51 — 16 ARG			
		221 P-45 — 41 LEU			232 P-42 — 46 SER		
	212 P-38 — 38 TYR					201 P-33 — 33 STOP	
	132 P-30 — 30 THR					121 P-25 — 25 ILE	
		101 P-21 — 17 ARG			112 P-18 — 22 ASN		
			220 P-11 — 40 LEU	233 P-12 — 47 SER			
200 P-7 — 32 TRP							213 P-0 — 39 TYR

Column 6, 6th Row

000 P-0 0 GLY					013 P-7 7 ASP
		220 P-11 40 LEU	233 P-12 47 SER		
	301 P-18 49 ARG			312 P-21 54 HIS	
	332 P-25 62 PRO			321 P-30 57 LEU	
	012 P-33 6 ASP			001 P-38 1 GLY	
	232 P-42 46 SER			221 P-46 41 LEU	
		313 P-51 55 HIS	300 P-52 48 ARG		
320 P-56 56 LEU					333 P-63 63 PRO

Column 6, 8th Row

333 P-63 63 PRO					320 P-56 56 LEU
		113 P-52 23 ASN	100 P-51 16 ARG		
	032 P-45 14 ALA			021 P-42 9 VAL	
	001 P-38 1 GLY			012 P-33 6 ASP	
	321 P-30 57 LEU			332 P-25 62 PRO	
	101 P-21 17 ARG			112 P-18 22 ASN	
		020 P-12 8 VAL	033 P-11 15 ALA		
013 P-7 7 ASP					000 P-0 0 GLY

Column 6, 7th Row

000 P-0 / 0 GLY					013 P-7 / 7 ASP
		033 P-11 / 15 ALA	020 P-12 / 8 VAL		
	301 P-18 / 49 ARG			312 P-21 / 54 HIS	
	332 P-25 / 62 PRO			321 P-30 / 57 LEU	
	012 P-33 / 6 ASP			001 P-38 / 1 GLY	
	021 P-42 / 9 VAL			032 P-45 / 14 ALA	
		313 P-51 / 55 HIS	300 P-52 / 48 ARG		
320 P-56 / 56 LEU					333 P-63 / 63 PRO

Column 6, 7th Row (reversed)

333 P-63 / 63 PRO					320 P-56 / 56 LEU
		300 P-52 / 48 ARG	313 P-51 / 55 HIS		
	032 P-45 / 14 ALA			021 P-42 / 9 VAL	
	001 P-38 / 1 GLY			012 P-33 / 6 ASP	
	321 P-30 / 57 LEU			332 P-25 / 62 PRO	
	312 P-21 / 54 HIS			301 P-18 / 49 ARG	
		020 P-12 / 8 VAL	033 P-11 / 15 ALA		
013 P-7 / 7 ASP					000 P-0 / 0 GLY

Made in the USA
Columbia, SC
08 December 2024

48730846R00073